MAKING THE MOST

of the

TEMPORARY EMPLOYMENT

MARKET

KAREN MENDENHALL

BETTERWAY BOOKS
Cincinnati, Ohio

Acknowledgments

Other temporaries for your comments and feedback.

Many employers, client companies, and coworkers for inspiration and information.

Temporary help companies and assignment coordinators who worked so hard to keep me working.

The National Association of Temporary Services (NATS) in Alexandria, Virginia.

The staff of the Columbus (Ohio) Metropolitan Library. Special thanks to Chris Nelson in the Media Center.

The outrageous, and extremely talented disc jockeys at WNCI Radio Station 97.9 FM—Columbus, Ohio's "Morning Zoo"—Shawn Ireland, John Cline, and Dave Calin.

Making the Most of the Temporary Employment Market. Copyright © 1993 by Karen Mendenhall. Printed and bound in the United States of America. All rights reserved. No part of this book may be reproduced in any form or by any electronic or mechanical means including information storage and retrieval systems without permission in writing from the publisher, except by a reviewer, who may quote brief passages in a review. Published by Betterway Books, an imprint of F&W Publications, Inc., 1507 Dana Avenue, Cincinnati, Ohio 45207. 1-800-289-0963. First edition.

---

97 96 95 94 93   5 4 3 2 1

Library of Congress Cataloging-in-Publication Data
Mendenhall, Karen, 1950-
    Making the most of the temporary employment market /
Karen Mendenhall.
      p. cm.
    Includes index.
    ISBN 1-55870-285-7 : $9.95
    1. Temporary employment. 2. Labor market. 3. Job hunting.
4. Employment agencies. I. Title.
HD5854.M46 1993   92-38566
650.14--dc20   CIP

To Eva Weisberg.
No one could ask for a "better" best friend.

Contents

1

Insights from the Trenches

Whether you are a CEO, a manager, a supervisor, a secretary, an attorney, a doctor, an accountant, a sales representative, a custodian, a food service worker, or a mail room clerk—no matter what your position in the hierarchy or on the corporate ladder—answer the following question:

What I dread most about going to work tomorrow is:

1. I might get fired.
2. The computer system or fax machine will break down.
3. We will run out of coffee.
4. The boss has found out about those personal long distance telephone calls I made.
5. I will have to meet, introduce, train, and/or work with, an employee from a temporary service. A "temp."

Your choice of 1, 2, 3, or 4 is understandable. However, the fact is that most people are at one time or another in contact with temporary workers. Because of popular misconceptions about temporary employees and lack of preparation (on the part of employers), most people dread the experience.

TEMPORARY SERVICES AFFECT EVERYONE

Imagine this scenario:

Your department is facing a tough deadline. Your secretary will go on maternity leave any day (actually, any minute would be more accurate). The receptionist starts vacation next week. The folks in the mail room have been complaining about being overburdened. Some people have been working long hours, skipping lunches, rescheduling vacations— and no one is happy about it.

So the decision has been made to call a temporary service.

Does the very thought of having a stranger do the work of your secretary make you nervous? Besides, there is the budget to be considered. Even though there is no viable alternative, temporary services are not free. You are very specific about the skill requirements, but you really don't feel comfortable about it.

Or this scenario:

Last month three district offices were closed down and seventeen people were laid off; you were one of the seventeen. Incredible. This can't be happening. After all, you have a degree and fifteen years of solid experience. Oh well, time to polish the résumé, scan the classified ads, and do some networking. Suddenly you realize that you are perspiring. In addition to that degree, all those years of experience, and a fabulous personality, you have a mortgage. That severance check won't last long. While you were living the good life, you didn't bother to save much, and your credit cards are maxed out. Your friends and relatives have all patted you on the back and assured you that you will find another great job real soon. Maybe. But maybe not. Probably not.

OK, so you can't relate to that, what about this one:

Your job is secure; you're a bigshot. All those years of paying your dues have paid off. You are sitting in your corner office with the great view, raring to go. Another day in the fast track. You call Jack, the Regional Executive Vice President of Special Administrative Projects and Development. You dial his number yourself (good for you). The line rings three times, then you hear it "roll over" to another telephone line. You get "voice mail." No, you don't want to leave a message on Jack's recording. So you punch the designated number that will connect you to someone with a pulse. A voice answers and you ask to speak to Jack.

"Jack?" the voice asks. "Do you know his last name or what department he works in?"

"Jack Smith. If he is not in, put me through to Mary Jones, his assistant. And tell her it's important." There is a pause, and you can hear other lines ringing in the background.

"Well, I'm sorry, sir. I'm a temporary and I just started." "I haven't met Mr. Smith, and there is no answer in his office. Ms. Jones is on another line. I can take a message if you will please hold on ..." Then you hear a dial tone. Your day is not going well at all.

Or this one:

You received your bank statement on Saturday and discovered that someone made a serious mistake — with your money. They are really lucky that today is Saturday, because you are ready to put on your boxing gloves. You put the statement in your briefcase and resolve to straighten this mess out first thing Monday morning. You proceed to try to have a decent weekend, but first you have to go to the ATM machine to withdraw some money. Surprise! The machine eats your card and prints out a nasty note on the receipt: "FUNDS NOT AVAILABLE." What?! That does it. You remember that the bank has a 24-hour customer service number. You go home and call.

A cheery voice answers: "Good afternoon! All People's Bank. This is John. How may I help you?" Through clenched teeth, you explain the problem. Then you are put on terminal hold ... and while you listen to that annoying background music, you think: "That was probably a trainee — or a temporary, which is even worse."

WHO IS THIS BOOK FOR?

So you think a book about temporary employment doesn't concern you? Think again. Regardless of where you work, what your position/title is, or even if you do not work at all — you have probably had contact, at some point, with a temporary. Chances are strong that you have spoken with a temporary on the telephone or that a temp cashed your check at the bank last week. Some of the correspondence that you received in the mail this week was typed, folded, sorted, and/or mailed by a temp. The x-ray technician who is going to take a picture of your chest next month when you have your physical exam—you guessed it. Another one.

Despite the expansion of temporary help companies and their services, many people don't know much about the world of temporary employment. Until they realize how directly they are affected, they aren't that interested. Even when a crisis situation crops up, the unfortunate fact is that few employers are prepared to work with a temporary. In addition, not many people are adequately prepared to do temporary assignment work, and no one, on either side of the coin, really looks forward to it. People have some strange ideas about temporary workers. That disturbs me, and I want to do something about it. I want to dispel the myths about temps and the negative stereotypes associated with them.

HAVING BEEN THERE

This book provides insight and solutions from someone in the trenches. I am going to talk about the realities of the temporary help services industry; the real ups and downs of the temp life. If you are now doing temp work, I'm going to give you some tips. Even if you have never done temp work, there is a chance that you might in the future.

And for you employers, I am going to show steps you can take that will guarantee you success when working with temporary employees. I am amazed at the simple things that employers fail to do; simple things that would minimize frustration and eliminate chaos, yet people don't bother because they usually don't plan on having to "deal with" temporaries. When things go wrong, they blame the temporary employee and/or the temporary help company.

I am going to show you how to make the experience a successful one for all concerned. Instead of rolling your eyes up into your head, pulling your hair out, and becoming more frustrated, you will breathe a sigh of relief. You will have peace of mind. My mission is to turn your temporary tribulations into triumphs.

WHY I WROTE THIS BOOK

In a previous permanent job I was responsible for "work flow coordination," which included assessing the need for and the acquisition of temporary workers. I was wined and dined by temporary help services, and wooed by departmental employees who wanted to hire temporary help. The thought of working as a temp never crossed my mind. Years later, as a temporary employee myself, I saw the situation from a different angle. Having been on both sides of the issue, I decided to write a book about the subject.

When I graduated from high school in 1968, I entered college with definite goals in mind. I knew exactly what I wanted to do, or so I thought. I majored in Journalism at a large university. I was going to (1) finish college, (2) get a fantastic position in the field of Public Relations, (3) get married, (4) replace Barbara Walters and, (5) have two perfect children—in that order. That was my plan.

I didn't do any of those things (as you know, Jane Pauley replaced Barbara Walters). After two quarters at college, I got side tracked, started working, and struck out on my own. I eventually returned to college at age twenty-six, and again at age thirty-nine, but I have been working in that nameless, faceless entity that we refer to as the business world for over twenty-two years.

I have had the following permanent jobs:

- Junior claims examiner at an insurance company (1 year)
- Stenographer/secretary at a large manufacturing corporation (2 years)
- Receptionist at an architectural firm (4 years)
- Secretary, later promoted to administrative assistant, for a government agency (4 years)
- Librarian/researcher/conference planner at a small non-profit association (3 years)
- Statistician with a government agency (1 year)
- Writer/marketing coordinator/trainer for the same government agency (3 years)

The above jobs total up to only eighteen years—how did I come up with a total of twenty-two years? Well, there were two summer office jobs before and after my first year of college. And for almost four years, seven months in 1985 and from 1989-1992, I did three things simultaneously. I attended college part time, operated a freelance word processing service and worked at temporary assignments. (I was and, as of this writing, I still am a "temp.")

In 1985 the non-profit organization where I was working experienced budget cuts and layoffs. Even though I saw it coming, the writing had been on the wall for months, I wasn't really prepared for it. I found myself unemployed and in need of income. So I registered with a temporary help service. I was put to work immediately and worked at temporary assignments for seven months straight while looking for another job.

After that, I accepted a job with a government agency and occasionally came into contact with temporaries. I stayed with that job for four years. In 1989, I decided to return to college, work on temporary assignments, and start a small computer/word processing service from my home. I felt good about my future and was enjoying my independence. Fate was on my side.

During the Christmas holiday season of 1989, I came down with the flu. I was working on a temporary assignment but I had to go home one afternoon because I got so sick. A couple of days later, I felt much better, and left my apartment feeling pretty good. I remember thinking "life is good, I am enjoying my assignment, I've made a lot of exciting plans, and I finally beat that nasty flu bug." I remember bouncing out of my apartment ready to plunge back into the world. As I think back now, I was probably on the verge of singing the theme song to "The Mary Tyler Moore Show" and throwing my hat up in the air, just like Mary Richards. I was smiling to myself about life in general as I walked towards the intersection and waited for the "WALK" signal. Yes indeed, fate was on my side.

And then fate spat in my face.

You have heard various versions of the expression "Life is strange. You never know what will happen — tomorrow you could step off a curb and get hit by a truck." That is *exactly* what happened to me that morning. No kidding — it's true. I'll spare you the grisly details, but suffice it to say I was seriously injured. I assure you that if you are ever feeling invincible, an experience like that will shatter such illusions. A tragic, freak accident is something you never really forget. The memory is still very vivid. Of course I remember the pain (a lot of pain), the ambulance, the police, the onlookers, the license plate number of the driver who hit me, and a lot of other things. But what I remember most is the first night in the hospital. In the middle of the night I was talking to someone on the telephone — sleep was out of the question. I remember saying out loud and to myself, "This wasn't supposed to happen." It wasn't part of my plan.

I went through a long period of time when I truly feared that I would never walk again, and if I did walk, I would certainly never walk like a "normal" person. Eventually, I went back to work and continued my college courses at night with crutches and an ugly leg brace. But I recovered — miraculously. And as time passed, my life took a different direction. There were a few more surprises in store for me, and I continued to work at temporary assignments for a much longer period of time than I had originally anticipated.

I didn't get the idea to write this book until early in 1991. I started to write a magazine article. I didn't have an outline and, in the beginning, I didn't do any research or interviews — all that came later. I just started to write. As I continued to work on temporary assignments, I continued to write. As I got further into the project, I realized that there was so much that needed to be said on the subject of temporary employment. I then wanted to solicit the opinions and experiences of others.

I'm not just some flake who can't hold down a decent job. Nor am I someone who has simply "dabbled" in temporary assignment work. At various points in my working life, I have worked as a temporary for many different reasons. Over the course of four years, I've registered with seventeen different temporary help services, which afforded me the opportunity to work at more than sixty different companies on job assignments ranging in length from a few hours to several months. Some of the assignments were wonderful, most were OK, and a few were absolutely horrible.

What types of companies have I worked for as a temp? Banks, insurance companies, law firms, government agencies, mortgage companies, a hospital, hotels, an encyclopedia company, investment firms, shoe manufacturers, a company that designs automobile decals, a retirement community, a cable television company, a philanthropic foundation, architects, engineers, and many others.

The city where I live and work is Columbus, Ohio. According to 1990 census figures, the city of Columbus has a population of 632,270; Franklin County, 961,437. There is a great diversity of business and industry here. And of course, we also have several large colleges, Ohio State University being the largest. If you have never heard of the late, great Woody Hayes and the OSU Buckeyes football team, don't admit it to anyone in this city. Columbus, the state capital, is frequently used as a test market by corporations when they are introducing new products. In the popular TV series "Family Ties," the fictional Keaton family lived in Columbus.

As a temporary employee working for businesses in and around central Ohio, I have been overworked, underworked, wined, dined, dumped on, ridiculed, abused, catered to, ignored, worshipped, and terrorized. Some employers have actually wept on my last day and given me farewell parties and lunches, others have begged for me to return. I have in fact made several "command performances." Some people have been glad to be rid of me, and one executive abruptly fired me in a very bizarre manner (I'll tell you about it later). I still have every time card from every job assignment.

Many people have asked me: "What's it like—being a temporary?" It is wonderful, exhilarating, rewarding, and challenging. And it is also horrible, demeaning, thankless, and boring. I have worked with many people who, to this day, I can honestly profess love and respect for. Occasionally we have lunch, exchange Christmas cards, call to say hello— that type of thing. And there are others whom I would love to personally escort to a torture chamber. I have had delicious fantasies about these nasty people getting fired and begging me to show them the ropes— the ins and outs of temporary employment.

I have firsthand knowledge of what really goes on behind the scenes. The life of a temp is not always an easy one. I know because I have been there. I have also discussed the situation with temporary help services, clients/employers, and other temporary workers of all levels: general manual laborers, file clerks, word processors, computer operators, administrative assistants, executive secretaries, accountants, custodians, and nurses/health care workers. And they all have some interesting (and surprising) things to say.

I want to correct some of the common misconceptions about temporary workers. I will say right up front that generally speaking, I think that temps have been given a bad rap.

EXPECT THE UNEXPECTED

This book is also intended as a guide for current and future temps. It contains lots of "insider information" and helpful tips.

You may now be thinking: "Gee — I would never do temporary assignment work. I'd starve first." Or you may feel pretty smug in your own position as a CEO, manager, secretary, or whatever. And working as a temporary or with a temporary may be the furthest thing from your mind.

I never planned on doing temp work (few people do). And I am sure that the majority of the client companies I have worked for did not expect ever to need my services.

I mentioned that I once was laid off from a job. Although it was no surprise, I actually expected to go out and find a comparable (or better) job within a few weeks. Really — I was that confident. But it didn't happen that way. It took a long time to get another decent job. And several years later, I never, ever dreamed I would resign from a very well-paying, secure job with great benefits simply because I didn't want to work there anymore and I wanted to do something different. But at the age of thirty-nine that is exactly what I did. I didn't quit in an angry huff. Sure, I was unhappy and dissatisfied and fed up about a lot of things that were not going to get any better. But I just knew the time had come for me to move on.

I was completely on my own. There was no husband pulling in a big salary, no rich lover (unfortunately), and no mysterious benefactor. I was not flat broke, but I did not have a fat bank account. I didn't tell anyone about my plan until I was actually ready to resign. I didn't want to hear: "Do you really know what you are doing?" or "Didn't that layoff and long jobless period teach you anything? Are you nuts? Have you forgotten about that whole experience six years ago?" No, I had not forgotten. I will never forget. But I also knew that I had to do what I had to do. I thought about it for two months and then I did it. I turned in my resignation, tightened my belt, made some adjustments, and proceeded to follow through with my plans.

One woman I know was unhappy with her permanent job as a departmental supervisor. In some respects, it was a good job. She even had a secretary whom she shared with one other staff member. She was dissatisfied for many understandable reasons and had made the decision to resign. After months of unsuccessfully hunting for a different permanent job, situations at her current job worsened. So she did some planning, turned in her resignation, took a day of vacation and signed up with two temporary help services. She explained to them that she wouldn't be ready to go to work for three weeks because she had given two weeks' notice and wanted to take a week off after leaving her permanent job. As soon as she was available, she was put to work. Of course she had to make some adjustments, but to her it was worth it. She eventually found another permanent job, but she told me that she never regretted her decision to resign from her job, and she was thankful that she had kept up with her skills.

I have heard similar stories from others. Here are a few:

I have two college degrees and a good track record. I was really secure. Then my company started trimming the fat — and I was considered excess baggage. I ended up temping for almost a year, and eventually accepted a position offered to me while on a temporary assignment.

My wife accepted a promotion, which made it necessary for us to move to another state. She is an executive, and I'm a factory worker. I temped at industrial jobs for eight months until I finally found another job.

My husband died from a heart attack while playing tennis at the age of forty-six. Unfortunately, I knew nothing about our finances, and I found out the hard way that we were almost broke. My daughter had just gotten married, and she and her husband were struggling. There was no life insurance, and his health insurance premiums had not been kept up. At the age of forty-three I had to learn to type, use computers, and answer phones. I hadn't worked in years. I registered with several temporary help services, and for a long time that was my sole source of income.

I live in California, and my family is in Columbus, Ohio. My mother was seriously ill, so I had to take a long-term leave of absence from my job in California. I stayed in Ohio for three months and worked at temp assignments. I couldn't stand just waiting at the hospital day in and day out. I wanted and needed to work. Mom eventually stabilized, things are OK, and I am preparing to return to California.

Maybe you feel you are too busy to concern yourself with a subject as seemingly trivial as temporary employees. Well, consider this: Some person among the ranks of your support staff might get sick, have a family emergency, or go on vacation, and maybe others already at the work site won't be able to do everything that needs to be done. Even if the organization operates with 100% perfect attendance 100% of the time (no one ever gets sick or takes a vacation—which I doubt), additional help may be needed for special projects.

Throughout this book you will hear some true stories about things that happened to me and to other temps on job assignments. Some are inspiring, some are amusing, and others are positively infuriating and disturbing. All of them are enlightening.

If you have been laid off (or flat out fired), I want to show you that it is not the end of the world. And if you are tired of the treadmill, rat race, power struggles, and endless games that people play, you *don't* have to put up with it. I want to show you there are other options.

You're going to learn some things. After reading this book, some of you will go out *tomorrow* and register for temporary work. And some of you will go in to work tomorrow and make a greater effort to do a good job—thanking your lucky stars for the job that you have, no matter how much you hate going in every day.

You will find yourself nodding, chuckling, and relating to many of the situations, observations, and anecdotes. In one form or another, you *will* recognize yourself or a situation. And you will undoubtedly gain a new perspective and hopefully a new respect for the temporary help industry and the "temps" who keep the wheels turning.

Enjoy!

2

Using Temporary Services

TEMPORARIES—THE NEW WORK FORCE

Since the mid-1980s, you have undoubtedly heard or read the following terms:

- Alternative staffing strategies
- Interim support services
- Contingent work force

Those are some of the terms businesses use to describe the multitudes of people who are employed on some type of "temporary" basis. It is important to point out that in this book, the term "temporary," as applied to employment, can mean a few hours/days/weeks, several months, a season, a year, or even longer, depending on the circumstances. Temporary does not mean part-time. A part-time employee works for a period of time less than the full work day or full work week. That can mean the person works half days for five days a week, full days for a few days a week, or some other schedule mutually agreed upon. A temporary assignment can—and often does—mean that a person is working forty hours a week (full-time), but on a temporary basis. In other words, that person is not a permanent employee of a particular client company. Many people are full-time temporary employees.

Companies hire temporaries for everything from computer programming to janitorial services to engineering. Instead of simply hiring temporaries as fill-ins until "more suitable" replacements can be found, temporary workers are regularly used as an effective device for management to help accomplish the goals and objectives of an organization.

GROWTH IN THE USE OF TEMPORARIES

Since 1980, the use of temporaries has almost tripled. According to the U.S. Bureau of Labor Statistics, in the early 1980s there were approximately 400,000 temporary workers in the United States. In 1986 the field of temporary employment services employed over 750,000 people on a daily basis. In 1988, that figure ballooned to over one million. The actual total could very well be much higher because the Bureau of Labor Statistics figure only accounts for workers hired through employment agencies and services for temporary workers. Excluded are people hired directly by employers on a contract or freelance, as needed basis. It is difficult to specify an exact figure.

According to the National Association of Temporary Services (NATS), Alexandria, Virginia, the temporary help industry has grown dramatically during the past two decades and has become a vibrant and integral component of the American workplace. However, a review of current industry statistics for the most recent three-year period (1989-1991) indicates that both industry payroll and the number of average daily temporary employees have declined. Despite this contradiction, temporary employment services regularly employ nearly one million temporary employees each day.

In the early 1980s, businesses in the United States spent over $5 billion a year for temporary services. According to NATS, the temporary help industry is responsible for an annual payroll in excess of $10 billion.

Any way you slice it, when we start talking about billions of dollars (with a "B") it's a lot of money. When one considers the growth pattern of the use of temporary services and the "hidden" temporary workers — independent contractors and freelancers—unaccounted for in the above statistics, the annual payroll for those who work as temporary help very likely exceeds that $10 billion figure.

You may be surprised to know that there are few, if any, industries which have not used the services of temporary employees at some point. Many organizations employ them on a regular basis. Banks, law firms, insurance companies, the hospitality industry (hotels, casinos, resorts, restaurants/ food service), hospitals, nursing homes, retirement communities, accounting firms, government agencies, and social services organizations are just a few. The list goes on and on.

A look in the yellow pages of the telephone book and in the newspaper will show a proliferation of temporary employment services, especially in larger cities. For example, the Columbus, Ohio Yellow Pages lists over seventy temporary help companies.

REASONS COMPANIES USE TEMPORARY SERVICES

Many factors are involved in this extraordinary growth.

- The changing economy.
- Skilled labor shortages—the technological revolution and computerization have created a serious demand for people with specialized skills.
- Cost reduction—temporaries aid efforts by management to reduce the risks and costs associated with recruiting and hiring permanent employees.
- Turnover—resignations, terminations, layoffs, deaths, and retirement.
- Declining company loyalty— more people are changing jobs more frequently. A certain amount of job hopping and upward, downward, or lateral mobility is now acceptable, forcing companies to do more hiring and training.
- The home office—an increasing number of employees are permitted to work from their homes. This often results in temporaries being called in intermittently to perform routine tasks that other permanent workers at the site don't have the time or skills to accomplish.
- Short- and long-term absenteeism—sick days, vacations, maternity, paternity, medical, disability, educational, and administrative leaves of absence.
- Job reassignment—sometimes permanent employees are temporarily reassigned to other departments or branches of an organization. Certain duties still need to be done, and people can only be spread so thin.
- Flexible work schedules—many organizations permit some form of flex time or job sharing.
- Work overflow.
- Special one-time projects— certain tasks are ideally suited to the use of temporary employees. Examples include conversion of documents to a different type of computer software program; assembling and mailing an annual report; distributing new product samples; addressing/mailing invitations, Christmas cards, or announcements about organizational changes.

- Highly confidential material — some projects are too sensitive to be passed on to others in the organization. Using a temporary is less risky because the temporary employee has no vested interest whatsoever in the situation. Sometimes management does not feel comfortable giving highly confidential or valuable material to even the most trusted employees in the organization.
- Expansion and business relocation — temporaries are sometimes hired to help set up new offices and keep the work flow going during the hiring process.
- Training of regular staff — if a company is making a change in equipment or switching to a new computer system, temporary employees who possess special skills can train the permanent staff and ease the transition period.
- Dull, repetitive, less desirable tasks — regular employees who are assigned to dull, monotonous jobs over long periods of time may become unhappy, and eventually their productivity decreases. Temporary employees, who are literally "in and out" over the course of a few days or weeks, often approach boring, less glamorous, less challenging jobs more philosophically.
- Emergencies and disasters — earthquakes, floods, fires, bankruptcies, takeovers, etc.

In addition to these legitimate reasons, there are other, less publicized reasons that companies call in extra, temporary help. Although few people would admit it, temps are sometimes called in to justify the need to hire extra, permanent staff. That way it appears that people are busier than they actually are — overloaded, bogged down, backlogged — whatever you want to call it. I have seen cases where temporaries are employed on a fairly consistent basis simply to justify the very existence of an entire department or section. It happens. Nervous managers are all too happy to request extra help and to see to it that there is plenty of work to keep the temps busy, or even to create work. I don't agree with that particular strategy — mainly because it reinforces the negative image of the temporary employees. Whether you and I like it or not, many people view covering themselves as the most important office commandment.

ADVANTAGES OF WORKING WITH A TEMPORARY HELP SERVICE

Some large companies have established an internal temporary work pool. They actually hire workers and put them on payroll on a temporary, contingent basis. However, most organizations prefer to hire temporary employees through temporary help services. The worker is employed and paid by the service. When a client company has a need for extra or interim help, they call and ask for certain types of skill levels, experience, and expertise.

This type of practice can reduce labor costs for the employer. They don't have to plow through piles of applications and résumés, interview dozens of applicants (either via telephone or in person), test them, or check their references. All this is done by the temporary help service. Granted, the organization has to invest some time in training; i.e., showing what needs to be done, etc.

However, the investment in time is not nearly as great, or as expensive, or as risky as it would be in the search for a permanent employee. Once again, the client company has the advantage. If the worker is not satisfactory, the company can simply call the temporary help service and get a replacement, call a different temporary service, or scratch the idea entirely—i.e., make do with whatever staff they have. The usual problems and unpleasantness associated with documentation, confrontation, grievances, disciplinary action, severance pay, and even potential lawsuits can be avoided entirely.

Some temporary employees become permanent employees of the client companies. In fact, some clients use temporaries to find permanent employees. The temporary job is then a sort of mutual testing ground, a trial marriage.

On more than half of the temporary assignments that I have worked, there has been at least one person who has mentioned to me that he or she was initially hired as a temporary.

Other advantages for the employer:

- No long-term commitment or obligation
- No time spent on personnel housekeeping: explaining the various health plans, retirement plan, evaluation procedures, policies regarding salary increases, etc.
- No bookkeeping or payroll

JOBS FOR WHICH COMPANIES HIRE TEMPORARIES

According to NATS, approximately 63% of temporary workers are hired as office support staff — secretaries, receptionists, word processors, various types of clerks, etc. This is probably no surprise. The remaining breakdown follows:

- 14% involve light and heavy industrial skills ranging from assembly line work to product demonstrations to janitorial services.
- 12% require technical and professional workers such as engineers, accountants, draftsmen, computer programmers, writers, lawyers, and managers.
- 11% are in the medical area, which includes registered and licensed practical nurses, therapists, nursing aides, orderlies, and lab technicians for hospital staffing and home health services.

3

Working as a Temporary Employee

Temporary workers used to be thought of as people who couldn't hold a job or who didn't want to work at a "real job," or as bored housewives who just wanted to earn some extra money for lipstick, school clothes, and Christmas shopping. Unfortunately, there are still many people who view temporary employees as transient zombies who happen to have a pulse and whose only mission in life is to rip off the business world by charging them for an extra fifteen minutes of work, earn a couple of paychecks, then sit home and watch daytime television until the money runs out. But things have changed somewhat.

WHO ARE THE TEMPORARY WORKERS?

There is no typical temporary worker. Temporaries range in age from teenagers who work after school or during summer vacations to yuppies in their twenties, thirties, and forties to retirees who want to keep busy and supplement their income.

Men and Women

When the temporary service industry was in its earlier stages, most workers were women and were employed to perform clerical tasks. This is most likely because they were filling in on jobs that were traditionally held by women. Today, things are very different.

In 1989, an independent research firm conducted a survey of 2,508 temporary employees for NATS indicating that 80% of those who completed a confidential questionnaire were women. It is true that most temporary workers are female. However, according to the 1991 Statistical Reference Index of the Congressional Information Service, approximately 60% of all temporary employees are women — that means that about 40% are men. The gap is not nearly as wide as some may think.

There are several reasons for this shift. First of all, more males are now working in jobs that are classified as clerical. More men are working as secretaries, file clerks, receptionists, word processors, etc.

Another factor is that more companies are involved in technical and professional services. These fields are still largely dominated by men, and many more companies are now requesting temporary employees to perform these tasks. Also, many men have chosen to enter the health care field, and temping in health care services is an excellent way to explore the opportunities in this field.

The 1989 NATS survey referred to earlier also indicated more interesting facts:

Temporaries are well educated:

- 82% have more than a high school education
- 47% have some college or business/trade school education
- 35% have college degrees
- 9% have graduate degrees, professional degrees, or graduate hours

Temporaries have gained new skills, especially computer skills:

- 67% have gained new skills
- 86% identify gaining computer skills
- 75% usually work in an office

Other significant findings:

- 44% provide the main source of income for their household
- 43% are married and of those, 80% have spouses who are employed full-time
- 54% have been asked to continue as a full-time employee where they were assigned
- 12% are retired from a full-time job

TEMPORARILY TEMPORARY

All kinds of people do temporary assignment work for various reasons. Here are some of these people and their reasons:

- People between jobs. Every day, people are fired, laid off, transferred, promoted, or get fed up with whatever or whoever, and quit their jobs, or move/relocate to another city. Temporary assignments help to pay the bills while looking for another permanent job. In March of 1992, the U.S. Department of Labor reported that the unemployment rate was 7.3%, higher than it had been for seven years. Over nine million people were out of work.
- Those who want to work temporarily. For various reasons, some people either cannot or have no desire to commit to a permanent job. This is especially true in the case of writers and performing artists, actors, dancers, singers, and musicians.
- Those who want to supplement their own income or their spouse's.
- Students. Full-time college students often work during spring break, summer vacations, and holiday seasons. Part-time college students are sometimes only available to work for a limited number of hours or days per week and appreciate the flexibility of temporary assignments.
- College interns.
- School teachers. Teachers often supplement their income by working during the summer months. Temporary assignments provide for this need with flexibility.
- Those who suffer from boredom. There are people who don't want/need to work at full-time, permanent jobs. They just want to get out of the house and into the world for a few days every now and then. There is nothing wrong with that.
- Those who want to keep up with skills, new trends, and recent developments in office equipment and computer software.
- Job hunters. Those who want to test the waters at various companies to find out about job openings and get a "foot in the door" sometimes use temporary employment to do so.

Many people like the concept of working for a temporary help service because their job assignments are arranged for them. They don't have to do the legwork of combing the classified ads, making telephone calls, sending résumés, and going back for second interviews.

PERMANENTLY TEMPORARY

Career Temps

Some temporary workers choose to remain "permanently temporary." There are many people who have built up such a great following that they don't want to give up the freedom and flexibility of temping. They are the "stars" of the industry. They possess top skills and excellent work records. Clients ask for them by name, and the temporary help companies bend over backwards to keep them happy by paying them what they are worth and treating them well because they want to retain their services. A great temp generates business.

Career temps (such as myself) are not working at temporary assignments "until something better comes along." Nor are we fretting and fawning and praying that someone will hire us.

Sometimes a person will register with one or more than one temporary help service and make a conscious decision to be a permanent temporary. Or, one can become "permanently temporary" by accident. I know one woman who registered with the local bar association with the intention of working as a legal secretary on temporary assignments until she found a permanent job. That was six years ago. This woman is in high demand, she is well-known throughout the legal community, and her schedule is always full. She does not sit at home waiting for the telephone to ring. Nor does she have to check in with services to ask for work. On the contrary, she has to turn people down frequently. Her skills and personality are great, and she makes continuous "command performances."

In order to be a successful temporary (especially a successful career temp) you must keep something in mind: flexibility and adaptability are essential qualities. If the idea of working at different places every so often and meeting/working with different people bothers you, you may not be cut out for temporary work. And if you always have to be part of a gang, group, clan, or clique, you may have a problem working on temporary assignments, especially short-term assignments. Even long-term assignments (such as maternity and medical leave replacements) come to an end.

Permanent temping is not necessarily for everyone. Whether you choose to work for temporary help companies or as an independent contractor, or even if you choose both avenues, keep in mind that no matter how much money you make or how much freedom temping provides, it is a different lifestyle than going to the same "safe" job every day.

Ask yourself these questions:

1. Do you readily adapt to new surroundings?
2. Do you find it easy to get along with various types of personalities on a regular basis?
3. Do you take criticism (justified or unjustified) and pettiness personally?
4. Are you a fast learner?
5. Do you work well under pressure?
6. Do you tend to get personally involved with coworkers?
7. Would it bother you to do things "their way" even if you know of a more efficient, less time-consuming, cheaper way?
8. Would it bother you to be supervised by people who are less experienced and/or less knowledgeable than you?
9. Can you honestly say that you manage your money well? (Regardless of how much or how little you earn.)
10. Do you consider yourself a winner?

Although there are no right or wrong answers to the questions above, if you answered YES to questions 1, 2, 4, 5, 9, and 10 and NO to 3, 6, 7, and 8, you probably have what it takes to be a successful long-term or permanent temporary. If you couldn't give a simple Yes or No answer to most of the questions, perhaps you should rethink your options. That doesn't mean you would be a lousy temporary employee. It simply means that you should consider it more carefully.

Suppose you feel you have the right stuff, and you sign up with a few temporary help companies. You have worked at several assignments and you realize this just might be the life for you. How do you know you have "made it"? Warning: It will creep up on you slowly. You will walk by bulletin boards in offices without even looking at the job postings. Then, one day, without even noticing, you will open the Sunday paper to the Arts section or the comics, and ignore the classified ads. You won't be able to remember the last time you sent out a résumé. Face it: you're hooked.

Professional Temps

According to NATS, although most (over 60%) of temporary workers are in the office support and clerical categories, in recent years there has been a tremendous escalation in the number of professional temporaries such as accountants, doctors, nurses, lawyers, and engineers. These professionals now comprise more than 20% of all temporary workers.

Many people, for one reason or another, do not want to be tied to one company. This is especially true in the case of skilled professionals, including doctors, chemists, lawyers, computer programmers, accountants, etc.

Skilled professionals who work at temporary assignments are most often referred to as consultants, and usually enter into a contract or some type of written working agreement with an employer. Although they are called consultants, they are, nonetheless, temporary workers, hired for a specified period of time, usually ranging from three months to a year, to perform certain services for a specified amount of money. At the end of the contract period, their contract may or may not be renewed or extended, depending on need, performance, budget, and the worker's availability. For many years I had a permanent job with a government agency that engaged in this practice of extending consultants' contracts on a regular basis.

FLOATERS

I've seen ads in the classified sections of various newspapers for floaters. A floater is not a temporary employee. A floater is a permanent employee of a particular company or organization. As such, a floater usually receives the same benefits and pay ranges of other permanent workers. The main difference is that a floater is sent to various departments and works for and with different people on an as needed basis.

This practice seems to be more common in large law firms, banks, and insurance companies. Some companies have an internal pool of floaters. There are advantages to working as a floater vs. working for a temporary service. In addition to a more attractive benefits package with items such as paid vacation, sick leave, and a health plan, a floater usually works for only one organization. It is less stressful not to have to learn new names and procedures every couple of weeks or months. A floater would have an edge over an outside temp with regard to upward mobility because the floater is already an employee of the company. Floaters' hours range from full-time (forty hours a week), to part-time (usually about twenty hours a week), to "on call" situations. There are some employers who prefer their floaters to stay home until someone calls and requests their services.

Depending on point of view, being a floater has some disadvantages that do not apply to the temporary employee. Unlike a temporary, a floater cannot call his service and ask for an assignment at another company. A floater usually cannot choose who she wants to work for, per se. There are limitations on the variety of job assignments, especially if the floater works in a secretarial pool or word processing department of a large organization. A floater cannot walk out of the building at the end of the assignment and leave it all behind forever. She has to come back soon and face the same music— whatever it may be. Although floaters are permanent employees, they are usually viewed as and sometimes treated like outsiders. I'm told that they often feel out of the loop.

Many floaters are cross-trained so that they can learn the specifics of various jobs and step in on short notice. There is no need to introduce them and show them where the copy machine is. However, some companies use temporary employees from a service together with internal floaters.

INDEPENDENT CONTRACTORS, FREELANCERS, AND HOME-BASED WORKERS

These are people who obtain and perform temporary job assignments strictly on their own, without the assistance of a temporary service. Businesses deal directly with them, and vice versa. They are self-employed.

At one end of the spectrum is the individual who has actually set up shop, maybe even rented office space, and through advertising and word of mouth has built up a steady stream of loyal clients. Sometimes these people employ their own support staffs. Businesses hire these independent contractors to perform certain duties. An oral or written contract is agreed upon, and the worker is paid directly by the client company. Often a fee which is lower than that charged by a temporary help service is agreed upon. This is an advantage for both sides. There is no "middle man."

At the other end is the person who occasionally types letters, résumés, reports, term papers, manuscripts, etc.. Usually there is a verbal or written agreement such as, "I will charge $_____ per page, payable when you receive the completed project." Or "I will perform the specified duties at your office for X period of time for $____." This type of free-lancer usually gets clients via word of mouth, and some-times advertises in college newsletters or sends out fliers and business cards.

I know of some people who do very well as independent contractors. But "doing well" requires building and main-taining of a steady clientele.

Payment

One disadvantage of working independently concerns the all important area of getting paid. When you work for a temporary help service, you can count on getting your pay-check on a regular basis.

I must say that almost all of the temporary help services I have worked for have had excellent payroll procedures. There was only one instance where my paycheck was lost in the mail, and the service reissued a check to me promptly. As long as they receive your time card on time, you should be fine. Many services allow you to fax your time card in to the payroll department if you are working for a client where you have access to a fax machine.

As a freelancer, you may have to wait longer to get paid. I have been fortunate in my independent, freelance assign-ments. I have been given a check or cash upon completion of the work. When I was paid cash, I always provided a receipt — for my tax/bookkeeping records and for the client's records. I never had to send anyone an invoice, although in a few cases I would have agreed to that arrangement.

I have, however, heard horror stories from others. Some-times they involve sending out second and third notices, being transferred to some myopic cadaver in the accounting department, or even taking more drastic collection action. I have heard about a few bad checks that were never made good. Aside from being aggravating, stressful, time con-suming, and expensive, taking legal action against clients doesn't usually build goodwill. The fact that the action is justified is usually irrelevant in the mind of the client. You may be reasonably certain that their version of the problem, if they haven't skipped town, will differ substantially from yours. There is also the possibility that the client is on the verge of filing bankruptcy. It happens every day.

Caution: It is not wise to quit your full-time job and strike out as a freelancer without doing your homework — especially if you are self-supporting and have no savings to fall back on if, or when, times get lean. Life may not turn out to be as great as you think it will; remember what I said earlier about things happening that "aren't supposed to happen." Earnings can be very erratic. It sounds good to say, "I have my own business," but I think that many people would agree with me when I say that starting, running, marketing, and maintaining your own small business requires lots of blood, sweat, tears, and, most of all — time. It is not for everyone.

It is difficult to build and maintain a steady clientele, especially when you run a one-person show, as was my case. Most clients still feel safer doing business with an established temporary help service, even though the services charge rates which are considerably higher than those charged by me and other independent contractors. The exceptions were people who already knew me and were familiar with my work. Even so, there have been instances when, due to other commitments, I simply was not available when they needed me. Most of the calls I received were from people who wanted someone on short notice for a very brief period of time: "Our secretary is sick, can you come in today?" or, "We need some help on a special emergency project for a couple of days, can you be here tomorrow?"

In the spring and summer of 1990, I received a considerable number of calls from companies and private individuals wanting me to perform various types of clerical support services, either from their offices or from my home.

In 1991 things slowed down considerably. I seldom received a call from anyone, despite continued marketing efforts. Many factors enter into any slowdown, but I personally feel that the increase in the number of people who have become computer literate had a great impact on my business and many similar ones.

Taxes

Independent contractors and freelancers are also responsible for adhering to tax laws and paying self-employment taxes. Be sure that you contact the Internal Revenue Service and other appropriate state and local tax offices. Your local library can also be helpful in providing information about tax laws and forms that need to be filed.

If you are seriously considering starting your own business, you can get some valuable information, advice, and assistance from the Small Business Administration. It is also a good idea to consult with an attorney.

THE CREAM OF THE CROP—A SPECIAL SALUTE

I would like to take a moment to salute some highly skilled professionals who may or may not consider themselves temporary employees: court reporters.

I have been called to serve on jury duty on two separate occasions; once in 1979, and again, ten years later, in 1989. As we know, the wheels of justice grind slowly. In 1989, during a long delay in a court case, I had the opportunity to talk with several court reporters about their work. They were very accommodating and I learned some things about the profession.

At another time, while filling in for a legal secretary who was on maternity leave, the attorneys I worked for hired independent court reporters to take depositions in the more informal office setting. Many court reporters chose to work full-time for a court reporting services company. Law firms use them on a regular basis. I have never heard one complaint about any of them. Other court reporters are permanent employees of a governmental unit or the court system, and they work at the same place every day.

Court reporters are in a class by themselves. Their skills have to be top notch. They cannot allow their minds to wander. Total concentration and extremely good listening skills are absolutely mandatory. No eating, drinking, smoking, nail buffing, etc. One small error can be disastrous. It takes a special type of person to master the art of court reporting. And it is my understanding that they are paid what they are worth—which is a lot.

If you have never had the opportunity to actually see these people in action, it would be worth giving up a lunch hour to go and sit in a courtroom (if you can find one in session during lunch) and just watch one. It is mesmerizing.

Court reporters get my vote for "The Cream of the Crop."

THE PROS AND CONS OF BEING A TEMPORARY

As with any career choice, there are positive and negative aspects to be considered.

I certainly don't want to scare anyone away, nor do I want to make false assurances. My purpose is to allow you to view the realities of temp life, and then make a more informed choice as either employer or employee.

First, let's talk about the good stuff.

Advantages

VARIETY. Working at different places and meeting different people can be interesting and is often downright exciting. You have the opportunity to learn about the operations of various types of businesses and to interact with all types of people at different levels.

CONTROL. You can choose when, where, for whom, and whether you want to work, and for how long. In that sense, you are in control of your destiny. You are not manipulated by any one employer. You don't owe any favors. There is no need to chalk up brownie points or kiss fanny and cater to various personal agendas. You give an honest day's work for an honest day's pay—period.

LEARNING A NEW TOWN. If you have recently moved to a new city, or if you are planning to move, temping gives you the opportunity to learn your way around and to become familiar with some of the industries, businesses, and people in the area.

JOB SEEKING. Maybe you are considering applying for a permanent job at a company. Temping gives you the opportunity to find out about openings and "test the waters." It can be a trial period and a learning experience; What does the company do? What is its mission? What is the line of authority? How is the working atmosphere? Is the workload distributed fairly? Do people really like working there or is it a soap opera?

EARNING MONEY. Temporary assignment work is more profitable than sitting at home watching television and getting depressed while waiting for the telephone to ring between interviews. When you are involuntarily out of work, you often have a love/hate relationship with your mailbox and your telephone. The mailbox can be intimidating because it often contains rejection letters and nasty past due notices from the utility companies and creditors. The ringing telephone produces anxiety because it might be a job offer, or it could be the collection department of the credit card company, (you told them you would mail the payment last week, but...). You quickly learn that the world did not stop turning simply because you lost your job. Life does goes on; you still have to eat and the bills still have to be paid. Receiving a paycheck for working and being productive at anything is much better for your self esteem and your budget than not working.

And then there is extra money — as opposed to money

needed to survive, pay creditors, and keep a roof over your head. I know of some people who have good permanent full-time jobs and have worked evenings, weekends, during vacations and holidays, or sometimes on a part-time basis at temp assignments to earn some extra cash. Even if you have a regular income, you can probably use extra cash for a vacation, a special gift, a new car or repairs to your old one, college tuition, new furniture, or to start a savings account. Temporary assignment work can provide this second income.

EDUCATION. I have absorbed a tremendous amount of knowledge about many different industries and businesses as a result of working temporary assignments. Keep in mind that the experience you get in one industry can and will help you to get other jobs—temporary and permanent.

You can also learn to operate different office equipment and become proficient on various computer software packages, with very little assistance. Some temporary services offer free training. Most training packages are computerized, user friendly, and easy to learn. Of course, you have to be willing to invest the time— several hours, days, weeks, or even months if you expect to become proficient. This is a good way to spend your time if you are between job assignments. It is to your benefit to take advantage of this added bonus. I highly recommend it. The more you learn, the more you earn.

SPECIALIZATION. Depending on your skill level and your experience, you can specialize. For example, if you are a top notch legal secretary, you can choose only to accept legal secretarial assignments. If you choose to specialize, you may have to be willing to deal with some gaps between assignments as your specialty may not always be in demand.

EGO. Whether you work at only a few job assignments or several dozen, information will pass your hands, eyes, and ears that will often be very exciting. You may be privy to details about lawsuits and settlements, company takeovers, correspondence to, from, and about celebrities, etc. This type of information is highly confidential, and *must* be regarded and treated accordingly. But you have knowledge of it. Having a finger on the pulse, even temporarily, can be an ego trip. The fact that the client and the temporary service trust you to handle sensitive matters is a compliment.

ROMANCE. This is one benefit that few people talk about. A well-kept secret. Before anyone gets the wrong idea, let me clarify that I am not advocating flirtations, illicit affairs, trysts, or rendezvous in the supply room. I am not suggesting that anyone sign up with a temporary help service for the sole purpose of finding Mr. or Ms. Right. But as a temporary employee working at many different places, it stands to reason that you are going to meet lots of different people during the course of the job assignment(s). I don't want to turn this book into a dating manual or a tawdry "True Confessions," but let me just say that this is one of the perks of temporary assignment work that should not be completely overlooked. How you interpret that and what you choose to do, or not do, about it is up to you.

A word of caution to both men and women: in today's stricter anti sexual-harassment environment, this still may not be a good idea. Make up your own minds about this and guide yourselves accordingly. You're on your own. I have brought up romance simply as something for you to think about.

Now that I have your attention, let's take a look at some other realities of temp life.

Disadvantages

PAY. The pay rate is usually comparable to the pay for similar work as a permanent employee; "comparable" meaning sometimes lower, often equal, and occasionally higher. Temporary help services differ in what they can and what they are willing to pay a worker, and the reasons for this disparity differ from service to service. However, a little comparative shopping will show that a person will never get rich simply by working for a temporary service. Yes, one can earn a living — whether that standard of living results in generic pantyhose or designer suits depends on skills, the job assignment itself, and the client company.

Geography is a factor in pay rates. New York City and cities on the West Coast appear to pay higher, rates in the Midwest are usually slightly lower, and they are even lower in the South. The cost of living in these areas is a critical factor. New York City is an expensive place to live, as is the West Coast.

Other factors that enter into pay rate are: skill level, the type of assignment, and the client company. Wages are set according to the job classification and skills. For example, you may get a high pay rate for executive secretarial work that requires top notch skills, but don't expect the same rate on a job assignment as a telemarketer or a file clerk — even if both assignments are in the same company.

There are companies that will say, "We don't care what it

costs — just get us a good worker, now!" Others adhere to strict budgetary limitations. They absolutely refuse to pay a temporary help service one cent over their ceiling amount. And they know that if they shop around, they will probably find a service that will charge them lower rates and send a temporary who is willing to work for peanuts — at least for awhile.

Your pay rate should be worked out with your service. If you feel it is unfair, speak up.

BENEFITS. The benefits packages range from small to nonexistent. The relationship between a temporary employee and her service is usually a "no work, no pay" arrangement. Some services offer holiday or vacation pay after you work a certain number of hours, on the condition that you work the day before and the day after the holiday. Others may offer some type of medical, dental, or vision coverage. But it is usually a stop-gap measure intended to give you some coverage between permanent jobs. Such coverage is usually expensive, and the benefits usually are not nearly as comprehensive as those offered by group health insurance plans. Many temporary help companies offer referral bonuses. If a worker generates business, either by referring an applicant for temporary assignment work or by referring a client to their particular temporary help company, the worker can earn a cash bonus.

Other benefits such as profit sharing and retirement plans are, to the best of my knowledge, nonexistent.

VARIETY. In the previous section I classified variety as an advantage. However, having to adapt to different duties and people every day, week, or month can be stressful. In some respects, it is like the first day of a new job, over and over again. Take a look at the variety I had to deal with over the course of a six-week period:

1. A two-day assignment at the offices of a very fancy accounting firm. I helped to collate some material for a publicity campaign. I was set up in the conference room, alone, and I sorted papers all day.
2. A two-week assignment as a receptionist in a very busy investment firm. The atmosphere was ultra professional, the switchboard was incredibly busy, and I barely had time to do anything besides answer and transfer calls.
3. A receptionist/secretary for a week and a half at a company that had color televisions everywhere. No kidding

— everyone had their own remote. The office was busy, and the atmosphere was more informal. Smoking was allowed everywhere, which is very unusual in these days of prohibited and/or restricted smoking.
4. A legal secretary in a law firm which redefined plush. It was the type of office where your feet sunk into the carpet, everyone whispered, and if you sneezed you felt like a clod.

Not only did I have to perform different duties at each of these companies, but at each one I had to learn new names, faces, idiosyncrasies, personal preferences, procedures, location(s) of supplies, rest rooms, fax machines, copy machines, etc. And virtually each one of them had completely different types of computer hardware and software.

Variety? You betcha.

STATUS. There is a stigma about being a "temp." People who have permanent jobs have a lot of strange preconceived ideas about temporary workers. Even if you show them your MBA from Harvard and explain that you are doing temporary work to fill the hours between interviews, you will be thought of as "just a temporary." Many people will ask you to your face, "Are you new here or are you just a temporary?" Get used to it. It happens a lot. Regardless of your education, experience, bloodline, connections, upbringing, capabilities, bank account, wardrobe, or zip code, you will occasionally be the object of ridicule, condescending remarks, and assumptions which are off base, at best.

ASSUMPTIONS. Some permanent employees will always assume that you want a permanent job at that company. If you do want a permanent position, this assumption is one thing. But suppose that is not the case. When you deny it, you begin to sound like Shakespeare's famous lady — you doth protest too much.

This is one of the most annoying aspects of working on temporary assignments. I have a real problem with it.

Whether you just won the state lottery and you are truly working just to have something to do, or you are waiting to hear about a job that you really want, or you are working on your doctorate, or even if you are facing eviction, the fact is it is no one else's business.

More realistically, suppose that you have several good years of work experience behind you; clerical, professional— whatever. You resigned from your last job because of the long commute, low pay, monster supervisor, office politics, job stress, lazy coworkers, boring duties, the need for change, midlife crisis, etc., and you decided to do temp work while earning your Master's degree. You are on an assignment as a word processor at a bank. Your background and area of future interest is botany.

The people at the job assignment are dropping hints about a permanent job opening for a data entry clerk in the investments department or a secretarial position in the human resources department.

Don't bother telling them you aren't interested. They won't believe you. First of all, no matter how nicely you say it, you will sound haughty. They will take offense and consider your lack of interest an insult. More than likely, one of two things will happen:

1. People will tell you in so many words — or with a look, which is worse, "Well, excuuuuuuse me. I was just trying to help you out. So much for gratitude." Then they will give you the iceberg treatment, quickly walk away, and mention the incident to others. Brrrrr! You may want to start bringing a sweater to work with you, because you will notice a definite chill in the air which has nothing to do with the weather or the air conditioning system.
2. They will listen to you quite intently, sometimes even hypnotically, and nod their heads in understanding. So you think the discussion is over. But after coffee break, those same people will bring you a blank employment application, and let you know the "inside scoop" on the best way to get hired!

When #2 happens (and it will) you may think: "Didn't these people listen to me. Am I not getting through?" Yes, they listened. And they heard you. *But they don't believe you.*

I racked my brain trying to figure out why permanent employees make such assumptions. I think I have figured it out: No matter how much people, in general, complain about their jobs, the fact is that they are glad to have those jobs. That job may be the best thing that ever happened to them. Even if they are miserable, they feel fortunate. Ergo, their thought process goes something like this: "I have a nice job and life is good. So, this poor, lowly temporary must really envy me and my station in life." That kind of arrogance, stated or implied, is really hard to stomach.

In discussions with other temps, the consensus is that there is an arrogance and a smugness that prevail among permanent employees, from one end of the hierarchy to the other. As one temp said to me, "These people and their egos really slay me. Their attitude is, `If you are really good, and if you jump through any and all hoops, we might think about letting you work here.' What a bunch of tripe."

CONDESCENDING, PATRONIZING REMARKS. For example, you are working on a two-week assignment. During the second week, your supervisor says, "Maybe we can find something for you to do for a few more days next week." (You poor thing.) My attitude about this is the assignment was for two weeks. If they need me for longer, and if I don't have another commitment, fine. But don't bother to "make work." I would rather call in and get another assignment.

Unfortunately, temporaries are often seen as similar to understudies for actors in a play just waiting in the wings for their big break so they can go on stage ...

RESENTMENT FROM PERMANENT EMPLOYEES. Many people who are firmly established in their "real" permanent positions are nonetheless bothered or threatened by the presence of temporary workers. This is especially true if they were not told much about the reason(s) that a temporary was being brought in. They speculate—loudly—"Supposedly the company is having tight money problems. Hiring freeze, hrmpf! If they have money to hire temporaries, why can't they somehow find the money for my raise/promotion, new computer, telephone system, paper clips, etc.?" Or you may hear, "It is interesting that they are bringing in extra help. Aren't they satisfied with the way we are doing things? I know how to do my job. Besides, I could use the overtime pay."

Permanent employees of all levels often make assumptions about what the temporary employees are being paid. Invoices from the temporary help service are sent to the client company every week. Eventually some people find out what the service is charging the company. Some of these uninformed individuals assume that the temp receives the full amount—they don't know that the service takes a cut. Strangely enough, management and supervisors seem to harbor the strongest resentment about what the temp is being paid, or what they assume the temp is being paid. It doesn't matter how efficient the temp is, how many people's jobs she is required to perform, or how little she is actually being paid, the fact that the company is being charged for services rendered really bothers some people.

On a couple of occasions, after being reminded that "We are paying you $_____," I have had to educate some people about how things really are. I never, ever, specify what I actually earn on any assignment. That is no one's business, but I let them know that "*they* are not paying me $_____. The temporary help service pays me after taking a cut of whatever they are charging the company." I have also pointed out (diplomatically, of course) that I felt I was doing a good job, but if they felt they were being overcharged they were free to get (and train) someone else, or leave the work undone. Believe it or not, they quickly backed down and become suddenly very apologetic— or at least quiet. In both instances, I happened to know that I was making much less than they would have paid a permanent employee for doing the same, or even considerably less, work. The employer was paying the temporary help company less than they would have had to pay a permanent employee. In addition, the permanent employee would have received a benefits package, which would have further increased the employer's cost.

LACK OF JOB SECURITY. Temporary assignments vary in length and dependability. Essentially, assignment lengths fall into four categories:

1. Short term. A few hours, a couple of days, a few weeks. These assignments cover short-term absenteeism, vacations, fill-in between resignations and new hires, and temporary work overflow or special projects.
2. Long term. For definition purposes in this book, I consider a long-term assignment to be one that lasts over a month, usually several months. Coverage for maternity and disability leaves fall into this category.
3. Indefinite. These assignments are open ended. They can last several weeks, months, a year, or longer. For whatever reason(s), the company either cannot or does not want to fill the position permanently. A client will often request a temporary to help out "indefinitely" while they are completing the hiring process, until some special project is complete, or until the money allocated for temporary services runs out.
4. Intermittent. This is the type of assignment wherein your services are used on an as needed basis. Companies usually request this type of service for help with work overflow and special projects, or seasonal work. They don't want, can't afford, or don't need someone for a full week or month. Usually, if they get a temp who works out well, they will ask for that person to come back. This happened to me several

times. There were times when I was available, and there were times when I wasn't.

LAST MINUTE CHANGES. There are no guarantees that your assignment will last as long as you were told. I once accepted what I was told by the temporary service and the client company would be a long-term, four-month assignment as a word processor. The organization had hired a dozen temporaries to perform various tasks for several months.

However, after working there for three weeks, all the temps were summoned to a meeting. The supervisor apologetically explained that due to budget restrictions and "reorganization," our next day of work would be our last. There was nothing the temporaries or their services could do about it. We had to move on.

A client company can "commit" to using a temp for a certain period of time, then abruptly reconsider and end the arrangement for any number of reasons—or for no reason at all. Sometimes, an internal employee is transferred into the position more quickly than was originally anticipated, or the hiring process is completed much sooner than was expected. Perhaps the client company decides to reevaluate the situation and the decision is made to divide the work among permanent staff due to budgetary considerations. It really doesn't matter; the bottom line is that you are out the door. It's over. The only thing you can do is get your time card signed, pack your tote bag, and leave.

The flip side of this coin is the assignment that turns out to go on longer than was expected. If you are happy with the assignment, this works out fine and it keeps steady paychecks coming in. But this can also be a problem if, for example, you made a commitment to fill in for a two-week period while the hiring process is completed. You have also accepted another assignment—perhaps a better assignment—from a different service which begins at the end of the two-week period.

Or maybe you don't like the assignment because the company is using you as dumpster for all the work that permanent employees don't want to do, or scut work that the employer doesn't want to ask the regular employees to do. In your eagerness to please, maybe you are actually handling the workload of two or three people. The company wants to keep you as a temporary because it is to their advantage, and they are going to get all the work they can out of you. They are saving money by not hiring and providing benefits to a permanent person. The temporary help service is also in business to make money and is not likely to beat up on an important client simply because one temporary is disgruntled.

In addition to changing the time parameters once an assignment has begun, a client can make a "commitment," then back out in midstream or at 5:00 P.M. on the day before you are scheduled to report to work. This can be really disheartening — I know. Here is an example from my own experience.

One service that I deal with really makes a Herculean effort to keep me working steadily when I am available. On the last day of a one-week assignment, they called me at 2:00 P.M. and asked if I would take an indefinite assignment which the client had said would last a minimum of six weeks. I accepted. Meanwhile, I contacted several other services I worked with and let them know that I had another commitment and would therefore be unavailable for at least six weeks.

When I got home at 6:00 P.M. there was a message on my answering machine. My assignment coordinator wanted me to call her at home as soon as possible. I sensed impending doom — and I was right. The client had canceled the order at 5:00 P.M., saying that they were going to reassess the budget and the need for a temporary. Clearly, someone had jumped the gun. Perhaps the person at the client company who placed the job order didn't obtain official approval—who knows? I was surprised, because this company was a large, well-known organization with a reputation for high standards.

Yes, indeed, that assignment definitely turned out to be "indefinite."

My service apologized profusely but there was absolutely nothing they could do about it. This happened on a Friday night, and put quite a damper on my weekend. First thing Monday morning I had no choice but to call the other services back and explain that I was available after all. After a few days of down time, I was sent on another assignment. But I had needed and counted on the assignment that had fallen through.

It simply isn't good form for a company to "jump the gun" as did the one in the above example. However, it really doesn't matter whether the clients changed their minds or if they simply don't have their act together. I remember engaging in some admittedly pointless speculation after this happened to me a few times, but it didn't change a thing. Lesson: Always try to have a backup plan.

UNFAIR SITUATIONS. If you are unhappy in an assignment due to what you perceive as an unfair or even abusive situation, stand up for yourself and talk to your service. Human nature being what it is, a service will often hear one version of a story from a temporary employee and another completely different version from the client company. People frequently see things and relay information in a way that will make them look good and feel good, even when they are dead wrong. And people sometimes tell lies. If others get hurt in the process, they will find some way to rationalize and justify their actions. That may not be a hot news flash to you, but it bears mentioning. Three different people might see a situation three different ways, depending on their own vested interests and agendas. When they relay their disparate versions of a situation to others, it doesn't necessarily mean that anyone is lying. It just means that each person sees the situation from a different perspective.

Enough philosophy. Back to the subject of being unhappy, or even abused, while working on a temporary assignment. Some services will go to bat for you and either release you from the assignment immediately or try to ease you out of it and into another one. Others, when they discover, or even sense, that you are not pleased with the assignment will be insulted. Sometimes an assignment which is unbearable for you, the temporary employee, is a win-win situation for the client and the service and will continue indefinitely if you allow it to. If you tolerate it for any length of time, it is your own fault. Move on as soon as you possibly can.

ANXIETIES: ADAPTABILITY AND SEPARATION. Working on temporary assignments can, in some ways, be compared to the first and last days on a job—any job—over and over and over again. Remember how you felt on your first day? Another comparison might be to try to remember how you felt if your family moved to a new area during the middle of the school year. It can be traumatic and downright scary. If you do temp work long enough, it does get easier, but there is always an adjustment period.

Then there is the separation anxiety. I must confess that this doesn't happen to me very often. There have been many job assignments where I have felt tremendous relief on the last day. As a temporary, I usually don't get that involved with or attached to people at the worksite. However, it does happen occasionally, and when I leave a really great group of people, it's sometimes tough to say goodbye. Of course, I might breathe a sigh of relief that I don't have to go back the next day and face the stacks of work and the day to day problems and hassles that come with any job. But I have felt genuine sadness more than once on leaving a job assignment. And much to my own surprise, I have, on occasion, shed a few tears on the last day. It creeps up on me, without any warning whatsoever.

As I am writing this particular chapter, I am working at a temp assignment that I really like. The workload is very heavy, the pace is hectic, but the people I am working for are... well, especially nice. We all really like each other. The assignment will end in a couple of weeks. I know it and they know it. The day will soon come when we shake hands and say goodbye. I doubt there will be any tears, but who knows? Maybe I will stop in to see them sometime, perhaps they will need me for another job assignment, but more than likely our paths will never cross again.

As I said, this is just something to consider. I'm a veteran temp who likes to consider myself immune to that kind of mush, but it occasionally happens.

There have been only two temporary job assignments that tore me apart when the time came to say goodbye. You'll read about one in Chapter 5 ("Hotel Heaven"). But another more recent experience caught me completely off guard.

In the fall of 1991 I accepted a three-day assignment as a legal secretary at a law firm. My service mentioned that this firm might also need someone to fill in later for a maternity leave, which would mean a long-term assignment (about three months). The client initially wanted the temporary service to send them three candidates to interview for the long-term assignment. However, after I filled the three-day assignment, the client spoke with me and an agreement was reached for me to come back in a month to begin training for the longer stint by working with the secretary whom I would be replacing. In the interim, I accepted a few short-term assignments.

When I started the long-term assignment, it became clear to me that I was not going to have an easy time. The training/learning process was difficult and there was an incredible volume of work. I felt that I was barely treading water. I didn't feel that I could handle the job, and I spoke to my service about the possibility of replacing me.

One particular day about three weeks into the assignment, everything that could go wrong did go wrong. I was overwhelmed with work, confused, frustrated, and ready to throw in the towel. I didn't just dislike coming to work — I hated it. I became upset and the attorney for whom I was working came out to speak with me. He said that he was very pleased with my work, and that he did not expect me to perform at the level of his regular secretary. I suggested that they get someone else to replace me—I told him I had already spoken to the service about it. He said: "I want you to stay. We all want you to stay because we like you. Promise me that if you get frustrated you will come talk to me first." I agreed to stay.

Things eased up somewhat. For the next few weeks I was OK. I still encountered some rough spots, but at least the situation was tolerable.

Then a strange thing happened. I began to like working there. I wasn't crazy about the actual job I was doing, and I did not want a permanent job at this particular place, but I began to feel comfortable—perhaps a little too comfortable.

One day in November the office manager spoke with me about my work schedule for the remainder of the assignment—especially during the holidays. This office manager was a very nice woman who treated me well. However, she clearly perceived me as "just a temporary"—a good temporary, but still an outsider. I had heard about a cocktail party/reception that they were having for clients in early December. She told me that I would only be expected to work until 3:00 the day of the party and that I could leave when they began to prepare for the festivities. She said that I could stay for a while and have some hors d'oeuvres, etc., but the invitation was hardly enthusiastic.

She then told me that they were having a luncheon as their office Christmas party several days before Christmas. She asked if I would answer the telephones while they were all out to lunch. She offered to get someone else to answer the phones and take messages while they were out since answering the phones wasn't my normal job. I told her that I didn't mind answering the phones, but I said something to the effect that I felt intentionally excluded from the holiday celebrations. She explained that reservations had been made a long time ago. (I know that reservations can be changed).

I agreed to answer the phones while they attended their luncheon but I told her that I would prefer to leave promptly at 3:00 on the day of the cocktail party. She mentioned that she and another employee had discussed the idea of taking me to lunch sometime before the assignment ended at the end of the year. I responded (not very enthusiastically) "Well ... we'll talk about it later."

OK, maybe I was being a sulking baby. Maybe the office manager took it upon herself to handle things. Then again, maybe the decision came from higher up. Maybe no one gave it a second thought. I really don't know. But ... I really had no one to blame but myself. I should never have allowed myself to get attached. Then I wouldn't have had expectations and I wouldn't have gotten my feelings hurt.

After that discussion with the office manager, I decided to begin the weaning process. I went in, did the work and more or less kept to myself. When the assignment ended, it was time for "Goodbye. Thank you. Nice knowing you. Thanks for helping out. Stop in sometime when you're in the area."

And that was that.

If you are human, and I am assuming that you are, you should know that temporary assignment work brings with it the risk of getting your heart broken, many times. But it is usually a "good" hurt; the recovery period is amazingly short, and the prognosis is excellent.

You have to be somewhat philosophical about it: it's the end of an assignment, not the end of a career, and certainly not the end of the world. You'll be fine, and so will the folks you are leaving behind. Be happy that you were fortunate enough to be matched with people to whom you hated to say goodbye.

One tip for getting through the last day(s) of an assignment that you really like: work even harder than you have been. One of my favorite terms is "cranking" (putting out a large volume of work in a short period of time). Any service that I have worked for knows what I am talking about. "Cranking" means that you go in, say hello, get your coffee, be extra nice to everyone, and make stacks of work disappear. No one hears a peep from you. And when you finish those stacks, you ask for more. Cranking can be therapeutic. Besides, it keeps you out of trouble.

Even if it was a crummy job assignment, on that last day, make an effort to bite the bullet. Be nice — even if you worked with a bunch of sniveling hypocrites who treated you like donkey dung. Consider this: they have to come back tomorrow; you don't.

4

Registering with a Temporary Service

THE NATIONAL ASSOCIATION OF TEMPORARY SERVICES

When you begin your search for a temporary employment service, whether as a potential employee or employer, check to see if the service is a member of The National Association of Temporary Services (NATS). NATS provides legal, legislative, regulatory, and industry-related activities, education, and information on behalf of its temporary help service members. Founded in 1966 as the Institute of Temporary Services, NATS is supported by more than 1,000 temporary help companies operating over 8,100 offices nationwide. NATS represents approximately 85% of the total industry sales, and has chapters in forty-one states and in Puerto Rico and Washington D.C.

NATS is the only national trade association devoted solely to the temporary help industry. While there are many temporary help companies, keep in mind that NATS members pledge to abide by all codes of good practices adopted by the association.

FINDING A TEMPORARY EMPLOYMENT SERVICE

You're ready to sign up for work.

For whatever combination of reasons, you have decided to sign up with a temporary help service. So you look at the ads in the newspaper. Be forewarned that temporary help companies run recruitment ads on a continuous basis in order to maintain a steady flow of applicants with diverse qualifications, and also to attract new clients. They may or may not have specific job openings at the time the ads are run, but an ad is an invitation—for applicants and client companies. Remember that not all temporary help companies advertise regularly. I know of some excellent ones that rarely advertise, and a few that never advertise.

So you grab the Yellow Pages and go to the "T's." Can't find it? Temporary help companies are found in the "E's," under "Employment Contractors — Temporary Help." Don't just start with "A," then "B," etc. The alphabet is not necessarily an indicator of a good temporary help company.

Try one of the large ones, one medium-sized service that is not so popular, and then maybe a small specialized service, if possible. I strongly recommend that you contact at least three different services. You can devote an entire day or more to registering with three or four different services.

If you work on temporary assignments for any length of time (more than a couple of months), you may find it necessary to register with more than one service in order to earn a living. When one assignment ends, the service you are with may not be able to provide you with another assignment immediately, and living several days/weeks at a time without paychecks is no fun. This is something to be prepared for. Registering with several services will give you a much better basis for comparison, make you more marketable, and thereby increase your chances of getting steady work.

A Sampling of Services

There is tremendous diversity in temporary help services, in all aspects: professionalism (or lack of), application process and testing procedures, pay rates, and quantity and quality of job assignments.

I compiled a log of temporary services and job assignments over the course of several years. It helped me at tax time and was an invaluable aid when I was writing this book—although that was not my original intention.

Listed below are seventeen different temporary help companies/services, a description of their operations, and the results of my interactions with them. I have purposely changed the sequence, the one I list first is not the one I worked with first, and so on. Also, the order of listing is not to be interpreted as any type of rating system.

Here are some excerpts from my notes:

LARGE, NATIONALLY KNOWN SERVICE. Fast paced, "boiler room" atmosphere. Assignment coordinators seem high pressure, anxious to put a body in a slot. They called me once, left a message on my machine. When I returned the call, the assignment coordinator told me the job was part-time (twenty hours a week). I passed up the assignment because I wanted full-time work. I checked in with them periodically over the course of three weeks, but they only offered mediocre assignments for a few days here and there in remote areas of the city.

TEMPORARY DIVISION OF A VERY LARGE EMPLOYMENT AGENCY. One job assignment was OK, the other was the pits. Their ads indicated that they were in need of people with word processing skills, but the jobs they sent me on involved typing on a typewriter. A typing test was given on a standard electric typewriter that was old and in need of repair. The temporary division did not have computers or word processing equipment in the office. They trusted the applicant's self assessment on computer and word processing proficiency and offered no testing of these skills. The pay rate was low. My dissatisfaction with them is partially attributable to their focus on permanent job placements.

TEMPORARY DIVISION OF A SMALLER EMPLOYMENT AGENCY. Extremely difficult to get through to assignment coordinators. Switchboard was very busy and I was often put on hold for long periods of time. Quality of assignments and pay rate were very good. Jobs sporadic — too many gaps. Coordinators made strong efforts to get good assignments for me.

SMALLER SPECIALIZED SERVICE. Too much paperwork during the application process. Was given various written tests, but no typing test or word processing test. All my assignments from this service required top notch skills. They took my word on my skill level and it worked out, but this policy concerned me. Quality of clientele, job assignments, and pay was excellent. Assignment coordinators were personable.

This service always sent me on very high quality job assignments and paid me well. My only problem with them was some down time. I had to move on to other job assignments with other services. Later I came back and reactivated. It took some time, but they sent me on several plum assignments. No doubt about it—their clientele is top notch. In addition, they offered good bonuses for referrals and for logging a specified number of hours.

SMALLER SERVICE. Called to make an appointment and was interviewed over the phone. I was told that I "had a good chance" of getting an assignment. They said that things were slow, but wanted me to come in to take a typing test. I never followed up.

SMALL SERVICE RUN VIA AN ANSWERING MACHINE. This type of setup is not, in itself, necessarily a problem. However, my calls were never returned promptly, and sometimes not returned at all. Although we agreed on several interview dates and times, they did not honor those commitments. I was told that someone would call the next day to confirm, and it just never happened. Tried to talk me into going on permanent job interviews, but at the time I wasn't interested.

This service ran a small newspaper ad in which they claimed to have many open job orders, but they never came through with any job assignments.

LARGE, NATIONALLY KNOWN SERVICE. High pressure, "boiler room" atmosphere. Spoke with a different placement coordinator each time I called in. High turnover among the staff. Kept me going with steady assignments during one seven-month period. Most of these were low level, general clerical positions. A couple of years later I reactivated my application and was not able to take word processing tests because the equipment was being used. I called twice to schedule another testing appointment. When I arrived for that appointment, I was kept waiting for over an hour, and had to leave without testing. I was never able to take the word processing tests. I accepted a couple of job assignments, but was not pleased with them. Because of the poor quality of job assignments, I moved on to another service.

SMALL SERVICE. Very good assignment coordinators. Conscientious about sending me on assignments where my skills would be utilized. Pay was fine. Supported me during a personal crisis (injury) and held the assignment for me. (They replaced me with another temporary and made it clear that she was filling in until I was able to return.) After one assignment ended, job orders became sporadic.

MEDIUM-SIZED SERVICE. This service regularly advertises and claims always to have an abundance of jobs. Application and testing process was standard. I called to check in a couple of times a week over the course of several weeks, and was more or less brushed off. The coordinator gave me the impression that she didn't want to be bothered and kept telling me that they didn't have anything.

SMALL SERVICE WITH A FEW SATELLITE OFFICES IN OTHER CITIES. Assignment coordinators were fine. Sent me on a low level, general clerical assignment with the promise that they would notify me when something better came in. They never did. This service advertises regularly and has a twenty-four hour number enabling interested applicants to call in and find out about various jobs (temporary and permanent) by punching a series of code numbers and listening to a recording. Pay rates were pathetically low.

SMALL SERVICE. Coordinator whom I worked with over the course of several months was very good. Tried to give me good, steady assignments. A few clients backed out at the last minute, which was not the fault of the service. A new coordinator was hired and we did not have good rapport. They began to send several temporaries to interview for one assignment.

LARGE SERVICE, NOT WELL KNOWN, WITH OFFICES NATIONWIDE. Application and testing process was very thorough. Coordinator made a strong effort to keep me working. Follow-up during and after the job assignment was a bit much. Calls were made several times a day to the supervisor to see how I was doing. This practice eased somewhat after I worked for them a while. Pay could have been better, especially in consideration of my skills and the length of time I worked for them. Several clients backed out at the last minute.

This service was very careful about getting the right match. They would tell me all they could about the job, people, and work atmosphere before sending me out. That helped a lot. I worked for this service intermittently for a long time, mainly because of the great personality and efficiency of the assignment coordinator. We had excellent rapport. But all the assignments were short term, ranging from a few days to a couple of weeks, and there were too many times when I was told that their clients changed their minds and canceled the job order at the last minute.

SMALL SERVICE. Application and testing were standard. Assignment coordinators were fine. Sent me on a low paying, high pressure assignment. The work atmosphere at this particular assignment was very uncomfortable. I never worked with this service again.

SMALL, LOW-KEY SERVICE WITH OFFICES NATIONWIDE. Application and testing procedures were more efficient than at many other services. Pleasant office atmosphere. Coordinators had great personalities. Pay rates quoted to me were also very good. I had high expectations about working with this service. But I was soon disappointed. Later in the day of the afternoon that I signed up with them, I was asked if I was interested in a one-day low level general clerical assignment. I was told that they didn't have any other specific information about the assignment, except that the client needed ten people. I declined and they said they understood, and would call me when a better assignment came in.

A couple of days later I called to check in, and was told there were no job assignments available. In addition, the coordinator confessed that the job offer mentioned above had been a prank. She said that they had received a request from a production company to round up ten temporaries and play a trick "a la `Candid Camera.'" The trick involved taking each temporary into a room, instructing him/her to get a folder from a file cabinet, at which time the "client" would leave the room and lock the door. At that point, the file cabinet drawers would open and peanuts would fly all over the room. The object was to videotape the reaction of the temps. The coordinator seemed to think this "would be a lot of fun." Maybe it would be — for some people. I forced a chuckle, then told her that I was more interested in a "real" job assignment.

Several days later I received a call from them about a job assignment. The information that I was given (the "specs") were sketchy. The pay rate and location were attractive to me, so I accepted the assignment. It turned out to be a bad experience. The service had given me incorrect information: the wrong software, the wrong address, the wrong floor, and the wrong name of the person who would be my supervisor. The people at the job site were unpleasant. Repetitive calls to the coordinators solved nothing. I terminated the assignment and my relationship with the service.

SMALL SERVICE WITH INDUSTRIAL CLERICAL FOCUS. Atmosphere was unprofessional. Staff stood around chatting aimlessly while I filled out applications and took tests. They just did not seem to be very busy. Much concern about whose turn it was to bring in doughnuts, who did what over the weekend, which stores were having the best sales, and where they were going to go to lunch. Coordinator who interviewed me seemed bored with her job. I was not given any blank time cards. Instead, I was told that their procedure is for the temporary worker to come in and sign an employment contract prior to going on a job assignment. I found this to be strange and somewhat inconvenient.

I checked in with them regularly for the next two months or so. The only job presented to me was a short-term assignment for which the client wanted to interview several applicants. This would have required me to take at least two hours off from another assignment without pay. I declined.

I continued to check in with them periodically over the course of several months, and was told that they didn't have anything, but that I had "first dibs" on the very next job order that came in. They never came through with anything, and I gave up and stopped calling them.

LARGE NATIONAL CHAIN. Application and testing procedures were thorough. Staff and office atmosphere were pleasant. Checked in several times, but they kept saying that things were slow. Might also mention that this service runs daily ads that indicate that they always have work and that they need word processors, secretaries, file clerks, and various types of other skilled clerical workers. They eventually offered me an assignment which required high skill levels, but the pay was pitifully low. I declined. They felt their pay scale was competitive, I disagreed. Then I was told that I did not score high enough on their tests to be sent on better paying assignments. I challenged this. They suggested that I come in and take the tests again. I didn't feel it would be worth it, so I moved on.

SMALL, LOW-KEY SERVICE. Staff was professional and pleasant. Excellent testing and screening procedures. Very good pay rates. They called me within a week, but I had another commitment.

As you can see, there is indeed a wide variety of temporary help services. I have had more success with the medium-sized and smaller services. But, depending on your skills, preferences, personality, and the general business climate, you may have better luck with the larger, nationally known chains or the smaller specialized services. I do believe that a successful experience depends partially on your rapport with your assignment coordinator(s). And they come and go — some leave large temporary help companies to go to smaller ones, and vice versa. I know of a few who have started their own services. Some were successful, others were not.

Naturally, it would be my preference always to secure interesting, diverse, challenging, high paying job assignments. Although many of the jobs I filled fell into those categories, in reality, "plum" job assignments are not always available. But that does not mean to imply that lower level jobs are not worth considering. As I have stated elsewhere, working, regardless of pay, is almost always better than not working.

There have been occasions when it was my preference to fill a lower level job assignment, often as a respite after completing a very stressful, albeit higher paying, long-term job assignment. I have been a paper sorter and an envelope stuffer. Other temporaries who are qualified to fill higher level assignments have accepted work assignments performing various tasks such as tagging merchandise and shredding papers.

Consider my friend Zach. He is a college graduate, and for nine years held a professional position in a large accounting firm. Zach decided to take a year off to write, and attempt to sell, a screenplay. During that time, he worked on temporary assignments as a custodian. Zach wanted to do some type of work that would enable him to contemplate various plot twists in his screenplay. He couldn't do that while crunching numbers and analyzing financial statements.

Remember: "Low level" and/or low paying jobs are certainly worth considering. They may sometimes have advantages that you haven't thought about.

PREPARING FOR YOUR APPOINTMENT

OK, you are ready to register for work, but you still have lots of questions. What should you expect? What should you be prepared to do? How should you dress? How much time will it take?

Do's and Don'ts

MAKE AN APPOINTMENT. Always call first and make an appointment. Some services have a policy of taking applications on a walk-in basis, on certain days, and during certain time frames. It is still better to call first to find out. You will be asked a few questions over the telephone about your skills, the type of work you want to do, and you will probably be told to bring your driver's license and social security card for identification and payroll purposes.

BE PREPARED TO SPEND SOME TIME. The application, testing, and interview process usually takes about two hours, so make sure you allow enough time. This is not a process for you to rush through on your lunch hour. And you certainly don't want to have to interrupt the testing or interview process to run downstairs and feed the parking meter.

DRESS PROFESSIONALLY. Dress the way you would if you were working in a professional office or going for a permanent job interview.

DON'T BRING YOUR CHILDREN OR YOUR PETS. You may think that doing so is harmless and cute. It's not. It is annoying, disruptive, and unprofessional. If your baby sitter cancels at the last minute, call the temporary service and reschedule. Make sure you call; simply not showing up is extremely bad form.

ACT PROFESSIONALLY. Don't eat, drink beverages, repair your nails, chew gum, or smoke while you are filling out the application and taking the tests. It just doesn't look good, and most work sites now prohibit or restrict smoking.

BE PREPARED FOR TESTING. When you arrive, be prepared to fill out a lot of forms and take several tests. Usually, temporary services give a spelling test, a filing test that determines your ability to alphabetize and put things in chronological order, a basic math skills test, and some sort of typing test on a typewriter and/or a computer.

I will share a secret with you: I absolutely despise typing tests. I don't just dislike them—I really hate them. I have tested as low as 41 words per minute (WPM) and as high as 107 WPM. Most services require a certain level of speed and proficiency before they will send you out on jobs. I can see the rationale—many client companies will routinely require a minimum typing speed of 50, 65, 70 WPM, etc., but feel the tests are limited in their usefulness.

In one of my permanent jobs I had the responsibility of testing clerical applicants. I devised my own tests. I did give a speed typing test, but I also required that the applicant set up a letter, correct spelling and punctuation errors, and type a memo within a certain amount of time. Of course typing *speed* is important, but how useful to your business is someone who can type 80 WPM if that person is unable to think or doesn't know how to communicate with people?

Other Considerations

POLICE CHECK OR CREDIT CHECK. Be aware that some services take your fingerprints and run police checks. In addition, some client companies require a credit report. The service is supposed to obtain your written permission prior to running a credit check on you. If you object to or even question this practice, be prepared for all types of rationale and justification — "security" reasons, "character" checks. Personally, I don't feel that my credit history is the business of any employer—particularly a temporary employer or its clients. You may want to think twice before you accept any position, temporary or permanent, with such a client company. Do you really want to work for people who can't keep their noses out of your finances?

INFORMATION TO BRING

In addition to your driver's license and social security card, you should have the following information written out in advance to take with you:

Your Educational History

Names and addresses of your high school, college(s), trade/technical schools, programs of study, your major, and the degree obtained. Keep in mind that verification may be requested.

Your Employment History

Names, addresses, and telephone numbers of companies for whom you have worked.

Names of your past supervisors and/or people whom you have permission to use as professional references.

Dates of your employment.

Reasons for leaving each job.

Make sure you are ready to explain why you resigned or were let go from your past jobs. If you have a relatively steady work history, or if you relocated, decided to stop working to raise a family, or returned to school, this will probably not be a problem. Also, staff reductions or budget cuts are not unusual. But I don't advise saying things like: "I was fired" or "office politics."

Don't go on and on about racism, sexual harassment, favoritism, jealousy, personality conflicts, power plays, or whatever. You make think you are being spunky; however, veracity notwithstanding, comments like these raise suspicion. This is neither the time nor the place to discuss these matters. You don't need to go into great detail about the reasons you left or were let go. Be brief. A job interview is not the forum in which to blow off steam and grind axes.

While I am on a roll, let me caution you against volunteering the fact that you filed a lawsuit against your employer or that some other type of investigation (sexual harassment, race/age discrimination, etc.) is pending. That is between you and your former employer. I was surprised to find out how many people willingly, and often eagerly, discuss these types of situations with prospective employers or current coworkers. Perhaps they need to vent or they feel they are "covering" themselves. I still don't think controversial situations such as these should be discussed with other employers or anyone else. You never know — someone may know someone who is friends with or related to someone at that former company, etc. People do talk. If you really get carried away, you might find yourself on the wrong end of a slander suit.

If you feel you have been discriminated against, you have every right to pursue action. Just don't broadcast—it's simply not a smart thing to do.

Your Résumé

Of course, if you have a current résumé—and you should —bring it and furnish it to the interviewer. You will still be required to supply similar information on their application form. And sometimes even the best résumés omit certain information which are needed. You don't want to have to take the time to look up addresses, names, and telephone numbers in the phone book. This may actually be impossible if many years have passed since your employment with the firms you are looking up.

INFORMATION TO STRESS

Basic Skills

You will need to provide as much information as possible about duties you are capable of performing. Included in this would be your ability to operate various types of office equipment including switchboard, fax, typewriter, CRT, computers, copiers, calculators, and Dictaphone.

Do not misrepresent your skills. Even if the service doesn't test you, you will eventually get caught. Don't say that you type 80 words per minute if your actual rate is 40. Don't profess to be proficient with WordPerfect if you have only worked on the Wang System. WordPerfect and Wang *are* both word processing packages, but they are *very* different.

Computer Skills

In discussing your computer abilities, be specific about hardware and software. Although certain computer software packages are very popular, be sure to let the service know if you are proficient with some of the programs that are not as popular. A good example would be Mass 11. This program is used in many architectural and engineering firms.

If you want to be sent on word processing assignments and you know several different software packages, the testing will take even more time. Each software test takes about twenty to thirty minutes. If you claim to be proficient on several computer software packages, some services will test you on each, so be prepared for this possibility.

Speaking of computer skills, like it or not, computers are here to stay. A glance through the classified section of a newspaper will show that most clerical and administrative positions require some level of computer literacy and competence. Even if you are not knowledgeable about computers, the person who is willing to learn computer skills has a definite edge over the person who is resistant. This applies to both temporary and permanent workers. People with computer skills are in much higher demand and are more marketable than people who can only use a typewriter.

Computer skills range from word processing and data entry to working with sophisticated spreadsheets to more specialized skills such as desktop publishing, database management, and computer aided design (CAD), which is common in architecture and engineering fields.

In 1989 I began to notice that most temporary services were using some type of computerized typing tests. (This trend may have started earlier—it's just that I happened to notice it when I reentered the temporary employment market in 1989.) Don't let this scare you. The tests are simple, and truly user friendly. I am proud to be a computer junkie, and I do want to mention that if you have never sat down in front of a computer, now would be a good time to do it. Don't wait until you are ready to take a test.

You don't have to be a computer whiz or go out and buy a fancy computer. Just familiarize yourself with the keyboard and don't be intimidated. It won't blow up or bite you —at least mine hasn't —yet. You will be pleasantly surprised to find out how much faster you can type on a computer keyboard once you try it. And you will love not having to reach for the correction fluid or look for the self correcting key.

Most public libraries and some colleges and universities have computers available for public use and offer free tutorials. Check out a few books and magazines from the library on computer literacy for beginners. Read them, then practice. Everyone has to start somewhere, and this is the age of technology.

I also suggest that you acquaint yourself with some people who are computer knowledgeable. I have found these people to be valuable sources of information. I used to love to pick their brains, and they taught me a lot. It may not be necessary for you to know how to build your own 386 40 meg hard drive, but it is definitely to your advantage to know some basic language and to know your way around a keyboard.

If you need to learn some additional skills, take advantage of any free training offered by your service. This is a good way to spend your down time and it will make you more marketable. If you are already a computer whiz, so much the better.

Legal Firm Experience

If you have very good skills and especially if you have any experience as a legal secretary, paralegal, receptionist, or "runner" for a law firm, call your local bar association in addition to registering with temporary help companies. They often place people in temporary assignments and also represent you for permanent placements. Many law firms use the bar association placement service on a regular basis. And the pay rates for these assignments are very good. You will have to go through the application, testing, and interview process, but the quality of job assignments offered is worth the extra trouble.

Special Skills

Don't forget to mention any unusual experience you have which provides you with special skills. Are you a competent trainer? Do you have telemarketing or product demonstration experience? Are you good at handling irate customers and clients? Do you have knowledge of any special terminology (medical, legal, architectural, etc.)? These are examples of special skills that you should tell the service about.

OTHER CONSIDERATIONS

Limitations and Restrictions

If you have any limitations concerning your availability or anything else, let the service know. Of course, limitations and restrictions will lessen your job assignment prospects. But don't worry — it is better to be up front about things. Just don't overdo it. For example, it would be foolish to say, "I will only accept high paying jobs, working with wealthy, good looking people who practice Transcendental Meditation. I don't answer phones or make copies. And I insist on free parking." Lotsa luck. I hope you like daytime television, because you will most likely have a considerable amount of free time on your hands. Legitimate examples of limitations include:

SCHEDULE LIMITATIONS:
- You can only work mornings.
- You cannot work on Fridays.

LOCATION LIMITATIONS:
- You rely on public transportation so you are only available to work in certain locations and during hours that buses/subways are running.

PHYSICAL LIMITATIONS, PERMANENT OR TEMPORARY:
- You need assignments that are wheelchair accessible.
- You have vision or hearing problems.
- You have mobility problems. (For a few months while recuperating from an injury, I had to let services know that I could not accept assignments that required me to climb stairs. During a routine fire drill at a job assignment I was permitted to take the elevator.)

SMOKING. If you absolutely cannot tolerate or are allergic to cigarette, pipe, or cigar smoke, tell your assignment coordinator that you can't go on job assignments where smoking is permitted. You don't want to be unpleasantly surprised.

On the other hand, you might be a smoker yourself. Maybe you only want to work in places that permit smoking (either at the desk or in restricted areas). However, in case you are not aware of it, most work sites do not permit smoking. Some have "designated areas," but many simply forbid smoking on the premises—period.

ATMOSPHERE. Maybe you are most comfortable in an informal, "blue jeans" working atmosphere where radios are playing. Or maybe you find that you are happier working in a very structured, professional environment where everyone wears suits and whispers quietly and only when necessary. This is information that your assignment coordinator will find helpful when trying to match you with a job assignment.

REGISTER WITH MORE THAN ONE SERVICE

I cannot overemphasize the importance of registering with more than one service. Perhaps a bad experience or lack of success with a particular temporary help company contributes to the negative image of doing temporary assignment work. But think of it this way; if you interview for a permanent job, and it doesn't work out or you never hear from the prospective employer, do you just give up and crawl in a hole and never apply for another job? Of course not. You persist. Often you have to send dozens of résumés, and go on a great many interviews until you get an offer and find the right match. If the first service you select keeps you happy, fine—but it never hurts to compare.

You may run into a situation where you pass all the tests with flying colors, the coordinator acts like your chum, applauds your skills and experience, and gives you a business card, with the exclamatory, "Oh, and I want to make sure I have your correct phone number. 555-1234? OK, great! It was nice meeting you! We'll find something for you, don't worry."

After you leave, you never hear from the service again. You check in periodically, but they don't offer you any job assignments. Move on. Don't waste too much time with a temporary help company that does not send you out on job assignments. And don't agonize over why (bad references?, bad breath?, etc.). Let them know why you are disappointed and try to get assignments with another service.

YOUR AVAILABILITY AND ACCESSIBILITY

So now you have been through the application process. Let the service know when you will be available to be sent on job assignments. If you are available *now*, don't hesitate to say so. They may have a client company who needs someone with your qualifications *today*. There is a chance they may want to send you somewhere this afternoon, or tomorrow morning. Or they may ask to call you when something matching your qualifications comes in.

Don't go home and stare at the telephone. Keep in touch. If you are not working, call at least once a day to check in. Make sure they can reach you. Remember— if you are out interviewing for jobs, having lunch with friends, running errands, or otherwise "hanging out," they can't reach you.

Answering Machines/Services

Obviously, there are times you cannot be around the phone when it rings. Despite the chagrin and extreme displeasure expressed by some people, I happen to think that an answering machine or some type of answering service is a necessity, especially if you have a very busy schedule, live alone, or have no one at your home during the day. The fact is that in this day and age, few people have lifestyles that enable them to sit by the telephone day and night in order to be available at the exact second another person wants to talk to them on the telephone. There are times when you are simply "unavailable."

I know this is frustrating. There are many times when I

wish I could wave my magic wand and people would be available to talk with, or listen to, me *right now*! But the world doesn't work that way.

Many people act personally offended because they think those who use answering machines use them as control mechanisms or screening devices. Even if this is true, to repeatedly dial a person's telephone number and hang up on their answering machine makes no sense whatsoever. If the caller can't say, "This is _____. Please call me," he really didn't want to talk to me anyway.

So, if you don't like answering machines, welcome to the age of technology. I don't like standing in line at the grocery store. I don't like humidity. I don't like traffic, etc. But I have to negotiate my way through these and many other unpleasant things on my way through life.

If you don't use an answering service or have an answering machine — get one. They're not that expensive. Avoid "cute" or distasteful announcements. Forget about limericks. This is no time to be funny or clever. Something simple is best. Give the basic information and leave it at that. Something like, "Hi, this is John/Jane Smith. Please leave a message after the tone and I will return your call as soon as possible. Thanks." Buy a machine that allows you to check messages from another location and learn to use it. Check it regularly for messages when you are not home— at least every couple of hours.

Sometimes a client needs an answer immediately and the service will be unable to wait for you to receive their message and return the call. If you are not available, they will look for, and find, someone else. Most services with which I have dealt will at least leave a message because they are aware that I check my machine regularly.

SPECIFICATIONS OF A JOB ASSIGNMENT

Specifications, "specs" for short, refer to the essential information that must be provided to the temporary worker by his/her service prior to acceptance of the job assignment. Most services will provide this information to you promptly. Some will give out partial information, usually because they are waiting for input from the client company. Unfortunately, others will hurriedly give sketchy information with instructions to report to a company and assurances that the details will be worked out later. "Go with the flow, everything will fall into place later."

The problem is that the flow often turns out to be a flood. Don't agree to accept the job assignment until you are provided with the following essential information:

- The name of the company. The complete address (street number, floor, department) and directions (even if you don't feel you need them).
- The name of the person to whom you are to report.
- The nature of the work and specific duties you will be required to perform. This information should be *specific*; answering telephones, typing—word processing or typewriter, filing, mail distribution, etc.
- The type of dress. Professional, casual, uniforms, etc.
- Your rate of pay. Surprisingly, some temporary help services, in their rush to fill the order, don't provide this vital information to the worker. And, even more surprisingly, some temps, eager and pleased to get the assignment, don't ask. There is enough to deal with without an unpleasant misunderstanding cropping up when your paycheck arrives.
- The working hours and lunch breaks. 8:00 to 4:30 with a half hour lunch, 8:45 to 5:45 with an hour lunch Monday thru Thursday, and 8:45 to 12:45 on Friday, etc.
- The length of the assignment. One day, two weeks, three months? This is one criterion about which you may have to be somewhat flexible. However, if you are filling in for someone who is going on a scheduled two-week vacation, you and your service can plan accordingly. But if you are replacing someone who has the flu, the client really does not know how long the assignment will last. You must allow some slack with regard to maternity leaves and long-term medical leaves. Neither the temporary service, the employer, nor the person you are replacing knows exactly how long they will need you. Maternity leave might be six to eight weeks, but the employer may want you to stay a few additional days to help out while the returning employee is readjusting to the office. The client should keep you and your service apprised of any change in plans. Permanent employees often return to work sooner than originally indicated. ("John's recovery from surgery is coming along faster than we expected. He may be returning the first week in July instead of mid-July. We will let you know for sure in a few days after we hear what his

doctor says.") Open-ended assignments are not the norm, but they do occur.

- Whether several temporaries are being interviewed for the same position. There is a growing trend among client companies to request that a service send them several candidates to interview for a temp assignment. Personally, I disagree with this procedure. While I can understand some of the rationale (test the "working chemistry," etc.) I feel that the temp has already gone through enough testing, screening, filling out of forms, and interviewing when she signed up with the service. I think it is unfair to send three or four people on what will be a wild goose chase and a wretched waste of time for most of them. Unless the assignment is an exceptionally attractive long-term one with high pay, good location, and a pleasant working atmosphere, I try to avoid these cattle calls.

For example, one service with which I was registered left me a message while I was working on another assignment for a different service. I check my answering machine for messages several times a day. When I returned their call, I was told that they had scheduled an interview for me with a client company for the following day. They were also sending four other temps to interview for the same assignment. This meant that I would have to take a couple hours off, without pay, to interview for a two-week assignment, at a pathetically low pay rate. I thanked them and told them I did not wish to be considered for that assignment. It just did not make sense.

You may be thinking that it would take forever to obtain all of this information. It doesn't. An efficient assignment coordinator can, and should, provide all of the above information to you in a matter of minutes. Sometimes, she may not have all the information at that exact moment, but she should call you back prior to finalizing the job order. That is her job. It is your job to make sure you have all the information *before* you accept the assignment.

There are a few temporary help services I work for that get an A+ when it comes to providing "specs." I rarely have to ask any questions, because the information is readily provided to me. Below is a generic example of how they operate. All names except mine have been changed:

On a Friday afternoon I was finishing a job assignment. Things had gone very well, and the service called me to see if I had a few minutes to discuss another job assignment. When I had the opportunity, I called and spoke with one of my favorite assignment coordinators. Here is how the conversation went:

"Hi, Karen. We have an assignment at XYZ, Inc. They need an Executive Secretary. You will be typing revisions and additions to a large policy manual, using WordPerfect 5.1. There may also be some correspondence for the Executive Director and you will have to answer the phone in his office, but the phone duty is not heavy. Standard professional dress. Your pay rate for this assignment will be $____. The hours are 8:00 A.M. until 4:30 P.M. with a half hour for lunch, and they would like for you to start on Monday. They have a cafeteria. Lunch and parking are provided free of charge. They are located at 123 Main Street, Building C. You are to park in the lot in back of Building C, go in the rear entrance, and ask at the front desk for John Jones. If he isn't in, ask for Bill Smith. The assignment will run for about a week—depending on how far you get with the project. The new permanent employee will be starting in two weeks, so it will not last any longer than that. We have worked with this company before. They are nice people, and we think you will be a great match. How about it?"

I replied: "Sounds good, Jane. I'm looking forward to it. I'll check in with you sometime Monday and let you know how it is going. Thanks."

This coordinator is really on the ball. Working with her is very satisfying. Even when things go wrong, she maintains her cool, and has cheered me up on many occasions. Everything went well. It was a "plum" assignment. All the specs given to me by the service were accurate. I did a good job, and the assignment ended. The client was happy, the service was happy, and I was happy.

That is how it should be.

In total contrast, I have, on a few occasions, made the mistake of accepting a job assignment without having all the specs. Sometimes, it was just a matter of waiting in the lobby or having a cup of coffee until the people at the work site got their act together. One particular experience turned out to be very upsetting—for me, for the temporary service, and for the client. I don't think there is any question about who was at fault. But let's see what you think.

I was going through a "dry spell," and I decided to try a temporary help company that I didn't know much about. I passed the interview and testing procedures with flying colors, and had a very pleasant talk with the coordinators. I emphasized that I wanted immediate work as job assignments from other services had been either sporadic or low level.

Within a few days, I received a message at about 2:00 P.M. on my answering machine. I returned the call and the receptionist at the service told me that they had an assignment to talk to me about. She asked me to call back later because she was the only one in the office at the time and she didn't have many details. When I called, the coordinators still had not returned. The receptionist gave me the information she had. She said that the job assignment was to start the next morning. She gave me the name of the company (a large, well-known company), and fleetingly mentioned something about working on Lotus. She wanted to know if I would report to the company the next morning. I agreed, on the condition that I be provided with the specs before the day was over. I was told that neither coordinator was in the office, but one of them would call me back by 6:00 P.M.

At 6:30 P.M. I had not received a call, and I had to go out. I did not feel comfortable about just "showing up" at a large office building, and I had no details about the job— who to report to, what floor, what my pay rate would be, what type of word processing software I would be working with, etc. I decided to call the service and leave a message on their machine that I would wait at home the next morning for them to call me and provide me with the information I needed. That way, it would be their responsibility, not mine, to explain to the client that I would be in later that morning. Much to my surprise, when I dialed the number, one of the coordinators answered. She told me that she had just walked in the door and mentioned that she and the other coordinator had spent the entire day working on some "really fun project" that involved setting up temporary workers in embarrassing situations and videotaping their reactions. The coordinators had been very excited about this project for several days, and it seemed to occupy most of their time. She said she didn't have time to tell me about my job assignment right at the moment, but she would call me back in about ten minutes. I wasn't very pleased, but I agreed to wait for her call. She did call me back, and we discussed the following:

- The name and location of the company. She said that it was on the 24th floor of a large office building in a huge downtown office complex.
- The hours. She said my hours would be 8:00 to 5:00

with an hour for lunch.

- Supervisor. She gave me the name of the person to report to (the person who would be my supervisor wouldn't be in until later in the day).
- Pay rate. I had to ask what my pay rate would be. She asked me to hold as she wasn't sure and would have to check. We confirmed the pay rate.
- Duties. I then asked her what type of word processing software I would be working on, and she said Lotus and probably WordPerfect. I explained that Lotus was a spreadsheet package, not a word processing package. She said that I could probably type letters by simply "pulling up Lotus." I found this to be very strange, because I know Lotus. It is a spreadsheet program, and you don't just punch a key, "pull it up," and type a letter. She said that I would also be helping another secretary to take employment applications and answer telephones.

This entire exchange was punctuated by the coordinator's giggling and repeated references to the video skits and the peanuts bursting from the filing cabinet. This was quite annoying because I had to ask her several times to bring her attention back to the issue at hand: my job assignment.

I was assured that this was an unusual situation — that they did not usually operate in such an unorganized manner, and that in the future I would always be given specific information in a more timely manner. Against my better judgment, I agreed to report to the job assignment the next morning.

I make it a habit to try to leave a little early on the morning of the first day of a new job assignment, and in this case it was a good thing. I had a little trouble finding the entrance to the building, even though I knew the downtown area very well. I went to the 24th floor. Several people gave me vacant looks, others raised their eyebrows, exchanged glances, and shrugged their shoulders. Someone suggested that I go to the 23rd floor. I finally found the office in which I was to work. The person to whom I was to report was not at her desk. Two other women were deeply engrossed in a conversation about freeway traffic jams, but acknowledged my presence after a few minutes. They told me to just stand there and wait for the person who had vacated her desk.

She soon appeared and told me about the office and what I would be doing. I was replacing someone who had transferred to another job in a different department. They needed a temporary to take up the slack while they searched for a permanent replacement. I was expected to work from 8:00 to 4:30 with a forty-five minute lunch. (Notice that this does not match what I had been told by the service.) The telephone system was explained rather hurriedly; there were a lot of idiosyncrasies, personal preferences, and exceptions to keep track of. As there were no written instructions, I started to take notes.

When I asked about the word processing software, I explained that I was told I would be using WordPerfect and Lotus. The woman with whom I was speaking snapped that she knew nothing about computers and that she had told the service to send someone who "knew computer." These are her exact words. To say that this woman was not computer literate is an understatement. *And* she was nasty. What was frustrating was her failure to grasp the concept that a person can be a computer genius, and still not be able to operate certain types of software. She did not know the difference between hardware and software—and this became a problem. She told me, "If you know computer, then you shouldn't have a problem. I told the service that we needed someone who knew computer." As you may know, "knowing computer," is quite different from "knowing French."

I went over to the desk, turned on the computer, brought up the main menu, and discovered that they did *not* have WordPerfect. The hardware itself was very nice. But I soon discovered that their software was inconsistent from station to station. On one computer they had Microsoft Word, Windows 3, and an accounting package. On the other machine they had DisplayWrite 2, Lotus 1-2-3 Version 3, and a database management program. What concerned me was that I was not proficient with Microsoft Word and I had never worked with DisplayWrite. The secretary told me "not to worry about it." She seemed more concerned about getting help with her other duties. That in itself was understandable, because it was a busy office. She also made it clear that she detested answering the telephones.

As we were exploring the computers, I began to make my impression of the work site. My impression of the company in general, and that department in particular, was a negative one. There were many people bustling about — and I do mean bustling — running, hair flying, talking with their hands on their hips, carrying papers, walking and talking very fast, with furrowed brows, flushed faces, looking very busy and making certain that everyone else noticed that they were busy. There was an aura of crisis and a general feeling of self importance and out of breath-ness. Get the picture?

I called the service and explained that there had been some miscommunication about the computer software. I also expressed displeasure about the atmosphere and the attitude of the people. We talked for awhile, and I reluctantly agreed to try to make a go of it.

That was a mistake. A big mistake. A very big mistake.

The next day, the supervisor told me not to worry about Lotus, since I "knew DisplayWrite." I had just started to learn DisplayWrite the day before on the first day of the job assignment. I told her I did not know DisplayWrite, but I was willing to try to do what I could. I found that Display-Write was not a complicated program compared to others I had used, and spent some time practicing by creating a document, retrieving documents that had been stored, and exploring. I explained to the supervisor that when I attempted to print anything, I had problems.

Knowing this, she asked me to revise a document which was stored on disk. She dropped a report on my desk, said, "Here. The former secretary typed this report. Clean it up and print it. I need it right away." Under normal circumstances, the task should have taken twenty minutes at the most. It ended up taking me a solid day and a half because when I printed the document, the fonts (type styles) went wild. Another secretary from a different floor who was proficient in DisplayWrite came and spent two hours working on the problem with me. She couldn't resolve the problem.

The suggestion was made to call the former secretary for assistance. The person who was supervising me was reluctant to call her and ask her any questions even though she was working in an adjacent building and had been gone only a couple of weeks.

The situation became more frustrating. So frustrating that I called my service several times and spoke with the coordinators. Various staff members came over and punched keys in an effort to "help." At one point, I had no fewer than seven people standing around me looking at the screen, pondering, scratching their heads. Eventually they all shrugged their shoulders and walked away (thank goodness).

When it comes to computers, a little knowledge is indeed a dangerous thing. During the course of a phone call to my service, I told the coordinators that I had asked for and looked for some type of instruction manual, and I was told that the office did not have a manual for DisplayWrite, and no one made any effort to try to locate one for me. Eventually, on my own, I obtained a manual from someone on another floor, but it provided no help. So I called the temporary help company again and said that it would be better for them to replace me.

The assignment coordinators suggested two options:

1. That I try to locate someone in the MIS (Management Information Systems) Department who could assist me.
2. That I come in at night (on my own time) and work on the DisplayWrite tutorial to try to learn the program. I pointed out that I should not have to do that and reminded them that another person who was proficient with DisplayWrite had not been able to solve the problem.

The next day, the former secretary was called, mainly because someone was looking for some documents that only she knew how to find. She came over, seemed very pleasant, and easily straightened out the problem I was having. It involved setting the fonts from a special menu she had created, something that neither I nor the secretary from upstairs could be expected to know. The procedure took less than one minute. I wrote down the command, and had no further problems with DisplayWrite or the fonts on the printer.

Meanwhile, I made several additional calls to the temporary help service and explained that the problem with the software was resolved. They were relieved. When I told them that the former secretary had been called, they seemed apprehensive. I was then told that my supervisor and the other secretary with whom I was working did not like her. Frankly, that did not interest me. I was simply trying to do a job, and I had a lot of work to do. Had she been called earlier, over a day of time could have been used more productively. The fact that she had come had solved the software problem. I breathed more easily—until the next day.

In addition to the printing problem, we had been having difficulty with the telephone. Some of the phones were not rolling over onto my line and I was therefore unable to answer them. The other office secretary became irritated. The supervisor also became irritated. This irritation escalated with time. The supervisor and the other secretary kept discussing the need to call telephone repair, but neither of them did so.

Meanwhile, I was getting negative reactions from people on all sides. Some people were displeased because they felt I was not answering phones fast enough (between the first and second ring) and others were angry because they felt I was picking them up too quickly and not giving them a chance to answer their own calls. It had been my understanding that the telephones were mainly the responsibility of the other secretary. I had been instructed to act as her backup.

About this time I realized that the rules and procedures were inconsistent. The supervisor confronted me and said that I appeared to be confused about the phones. I explained that I had been given mixed messages, that I had been told to assist the other secretary in answering the phones, but that it was primarily her responsibility. The supervisor didn't address that, but went on to say that it shouldn't be that hard. She said that she detected tension, that unless things were resolved the situation was not going to work out.

She reminded me of those who have just returned from some "assertiveness training" seminar and are determined to prove some point. She seemed bent on picking a fight in a professional, assertive manner. I was just as determined not to get involved in an argument. It just wasn't worth it to me. I was surprised that my efforts to do a good job and to help them with many other things did not seem to be appreciated. I became upset, explained that I was simply trying to do a good job and pointed out that the telephones themselves seemed to be malfunctioning and that their repair had not been dealt with. The discussion was ended.

During my lunch hour I called my service and told them about the latest incident. We concluded by agreeing that I would go back and finish out the day.

I had given my supervisor my time card that morning. At about 4:00 the other secretary told me that the supervisor (whose door was closed) was doing a termination and that I was not to interrupt her for any reason. I looked at the clock and mentioned that my time card had not been signed and that if the meeting was not over by 4:30 I would have to interrupt. The secretary was not pleased with my remark, and she repeated that I was not to interrupt. I called the service, and they said that instead of mailing my time card, I could bring it to their office next week (on my own time, of course) since this was a "special circumstance."

At about 4:15, a staff member asked me to type a memo. I explained that I wouldn't have time that day because I was in the middle of working on another project. She jerked it off the desk and said curtly that she would take it to another office and have someone else do it. At 4:20 my supervisor finished her meeting, signed my time card, and gave it to me.

Frankly, when I left the office, I wasn't sure whether I wanted to go back. The experience seemed to be more trouble than what it was worth, for all concerned.

I also made the mistake of allowing the situation to ruin my weekend. I was upset about it. The idea of going back to that place made me ill. But on Monday morning, like a trouper, I went back. I had quite a bit of typing to do. I had noticed the previous Friday that whenever someone gave something of any length to the other secretary to type, she would say, "Give it to Karen. She is doing all the typing now." On Monday, things didn't go much better. The atmosphere was not pleasant. I called the service again and told them I couldn't stand it. They said: "Try to stick it out. And call us as often as you want if you need to blow off steam." Thanks a lot.

Within a few hours, I could take no more. I became very upset and knew that I could not work there any longer. I terminated the assignment that morning and asked the service to mail my paycheck for the hours I had worked.

A few days later, I spoke to the coordinator at the service about the entire incident. After much more pointless discussion, we mutually agreed that it would be best to terminate our relationship.

That was an example of what happens when no specifications or incorrect specifications are provided and the temporary employee is incorrectly assigned. There were several issues involved in this assignment that made it difficult for the temporary worker.

The first problem was at the client company. The person who placed the job order was focused on getting assistance with her duties. She knew nothing about computer software or about the requirements of the actual job the temporary employee would be doing. My initial concerns about not knowing DisplayWrite turned out to be minimal. The problem with the software was not a matter of my inexperience with the program, because their system had been customized. Remember that the woman who came from another floor to help me was very proficient with DisplayWrite and was unable to solve the problem. The people I was working with simply did not want to call the former secretary because of "office politics" and undercurrents.

The second problem was with the service. The assignment coordinator should have waited until specific information was provided on the computer software. The service should have explained the importance of matching the client's needs with the skills and capabilities of the temporary employee. They could have explained that they had many competent people waiting to go to work, but that more specific information about the assignment was needed. At the time, their priority was the hidden video project and the peanuts flying out of a file cabinet drawer. They took a gamble. This was a big client. They were still giddy from playing "Candid Camera," and they didn't want to take the chance that the client would call another service.

The third problem was with me. I should not have accepted the assignment without more information. Had I paid attention to my initial concerns, I could have avoided the whole thing.

Believe it or not, this assignment was not the worst I have ever had, but it was one of the most frustrating and upsetting. I felt that the temporary help company let me down. I had told them that they should send someone else, and give me another assignment. The attitude of the coordinators was "we have a warm body in a slot, we're earning a commission, and the client isn't complaining." The fact that the situation could have been prevented made it even more upsetting. This was a terrible way for a service to begin a working relationship with a new temporary employee. It was the beginning and the end of our relationship and should not have happened in the first place.

How do you see it? It occurs to me that an outsider may view this situation differently. I have received a few dissenting opinions about this experience. The consensus was that the service did indeed bungle the job order, from the beginning, and that if they lost a client it was their own fault. But there is some disagreement as to whether or not I could have handled the situation better.

One person felt that since I had crossed several hurdles already, I should have stuck with it until something better came along. I must admit that when I terminated this assignment, it resulted in a financial hardship because I didn't get another assignment from any other service for awhile. This had nothing to do with my leaving the assignment as the other services were not aware of what had happened. I wasn't being "blackballed"; it was just poor timing. Things were slow for several weeks.

A few other people felt that I should have specifically stated, "I will work until the end of the day/week, but I want out of this assignment." In retrospect, I see that this is good advice. I have learned that it is important to set my limits with a service, rather than simply asking them to replace me. By giving them a deadline, it establishes my need to leave the job, takes care of me, my service, and their client. This is a win-win situation. I have provided the service with enough time to find a replacement and thereby satisfy the customer, and I have chosen not to remain in a situation that is unbearable to me.

CHECKLIST FOR TEMPORARY EMPLOYEES

Let's pull it all together. Make certain you know the following before you accept a job assignment:

_____ Exact location of the work site.

_____ Your supervisor's name, correct spelling, pronunciation, and gender (Mr., Mrs., or Ms.).

_____ Specific duties you will be performing.

_____ Your working hours.

_____ Your exact pay rate, not an approximation.

_____ Length of the assignment. Remember, you are making a commitment—not just passing the time until something better comes along.

_____ Expected attire. Suits, dresses, blue jeans, sweats?

_____ Type of equipment you will be using.

_____ If the job requires computer work, what type of hardware and software will you be using?

5

Reporting for Work

To a great extent, your success or failure as a temporary will depend on one person—you. Here are some helpful "insider tips" that will make your life a lot easier.

BE PROFESSIONAL

Punctuality and Attendance

Always arrive a few minutes early, don't take extended lunches, and work until quitting time. You will probably see others (regular permanent employees) sliding in late, taking long lunches/breaks, turning off equipment fifteen minutes before quitting time, and leaving early. You may think to yourself: "It's not right and it's not fair." You are right. But, so what? Ignore it and don't comment about it—even if you are prompted to do so. Forget about it. That is not your business. You are being paid to work a specified number of hours. Do so and let others worry about their schedules.

At most temporary job assignments where I have worked, at least a few people were already at the office regardless of how early I arrived. But there have been some jobs where I could not get into the building until someone else arrived to unlock the doors—usually ten to fifteen minutes late. Sometimes I waited as long as a half hour. Did I go to a restaurant and order breakfast? Nope. I waited. The client was charged for the full eight hours because I was there available for work. The fact that I was unable to enter the office was their fault.

I realize that temporaries get sick and encounter various emergencies (car trouble, late buses, sick children, leaky roofs, etc.). Despite some opinions to the contrary, temporary employees are human beings with human problems. But your service is not going to take kindly to any absenteeism, and the client's reaction will range from conditional tolerance to fury. This is certainly not the time to play hooky—calling in sick when you really want to stay home and catch up on the soaps or some much needed sleep.

If you do have an emergency, call your temporary help service as soon as possible. Most of them have twenty-four hour answering services or at least answering machines that are turned on when the offices close for the day. Sometimes you may even be given the home telephone number of your assignment coordinator.

Keep in mind, though, that even if your absenteeism is unavoidable, you run the risk of being replaced. And the client may decide to go to another service. Some companies are understanding and some are not. That is the nature of the temporary service business.

Try to schedule appointments (medical, dental, etc.) during your lunch hour. I know sometimes this is impossible, but if you have been at the assignment awhile, maybe something can be worked out with your supervisor at the work site. If you have a rare supervisor who offers to give you this time off with pay, thank her for the offer, but always make the time up or deduct it from your time card. Offer to work through your lunch hour the next day or to make up the time some other way. Some client companies can be very understanding, and others simply do not tolerate any deviations whatsoever.

Personal Telephone Calls

Discourage—or forbid — your spouse, lover, friends, children, doctor, lawyer, minister, rabbi, and creditors from calling you on the job. Remember, this is why you installed an answering machine at home. Your assignment coordinator should know how to reach you in case of emergency, but should call only in the case of a real emergency. Some services will call you, in addition to your supervisor, to see how things are going. But those are usually very short calls. Of course, when the end of the assignment is near, you want to check in with your service. I advise making the call from a pay telephone during your lunch hour. One temporary help service that I have worked for is very discreet about calling me. My coordinator always asks: "Can you give us a call at lunch? We have another job assignment to run by you."

The temporary help companies don't want to hear complaints from clients about you tying up the telephone lines and wasting their time and their dollars. This is not the time to call and chat with your friends, find out the status of your credit card account, or follow up on job leads. Many people will wave a hand and say, "Go ahead and use the phones. No problem." But they aren't crazy about their permanent employees making and receiving personal telephone calls, so imagine how they really feel about a temporary doing so.

On rare occasions I have had to use the telephone at a job site to make a personal telephone call. I don't like the idea of doing it, but sometimes you have no choice. *Always* charge personal long distance calls to your home telephone number. That's what long distance calling cards are for. They also come in handy when you find yourself at a pay telephone without a quarter. If you don't have a calling card, get one. And use it.

If you *ever* make a long distance personal call at the expense of the client company, you deserve whatever repercussions follow. You may think you are slick, but don't kid yourself. Telephone bills and computer printouts reveal all kinds of things. That is stealing, and you deserve to get caught. I just might find you and beat you over the head with this book.

Equipment and Supplies

Exercise care when using the equipment and supplies at the client company. Don't be afraid of a fancy copy machine, but make sure you know how to use it, and what to do if it jams. Whether it is a copy machine, a Dictaphone, a stapler, or a coffee cup, don't slam/bang things around. If you have a problem with a piece of equipment, read the directions/manual, or let someone know. They will see that you get help. If you are using someone else's desk, make sure you leave it as neat as you found it — preferably neater. Accidents happen (coffee spills, etc.) and temporaries are human. If it happens to you, apologize, and do what you can to remedy the situation. Then get right back to work.

Work Area

Your work area may not be perfect, but as long as it is functional, don't grumble. If you need something (scissors, a typing/copy stand, etc.) just ask. They will probably try to accommodate you because they want you to get the work done. You should say something about your work area if you are asked to work in extremely dirty or dusty areas that are bad for the eyes, the respiratory system, and the clothes or with loud — and I mean really LOUD — noise that makes concentration impossible. If the noise is so bad that you can't hear the Dictaphone or the caller on the other end of the line, you should say something, as tactfully as possible.

Complaints of Others

If you hear someone making a nasty comment about your work performance to someone else, don't ignore it. Go to the person who made the comment and gently say, "Could you please show me what I did wrong. It would help me if you show me the correct way to do it, and I will do my best not to make the same mistake again." If this is said in a nice tone with no trace of sarcasm, it can work wonders. In my experience, the complainer may actually apologize. If so, graciously accept the apology.

The trick to making this particular tactic work is not to discuss it later with others at the job site. Someone will probably come up to you and whisper: "I was so glad you stood up for yourself. She deserves to be put in her place. Good for you; we were cheering you on." *Do not comment.* This will be a good exercise to help you perfect the art of saying nothing when there is nothing more to be said.

Your Complaints

Don't be a chronic complainer. Learn to ignore minor inconveniences and idiosyncrasies. People are people. You should not be complaining to your supervisor or calling your service to whine about the annoying whistling and gum chewing of the person sitting next to you, the lack of privacy in the lunch room, or the selection in the vending machines.

I was filling a job assignment that involved typing information from claim forms into a computer. Period. The work was very mundane. The first few days I noticed that everyone in that work area wore headphones. I assumed that they were transcribing from Dictaphones. In the ladies' room I ran into another temporary who complained that the other workers were listening to radios. This bothered her because she felt that it was unprofessional. (Maybe she was really bothered because she had no portable radio or headphones.)

It occurred to me that the supervisors of this department made a smart decision in permitting workers to listen to the radio as long as it did not disturb the work flow or anyone's concentration. The area was isolated and there was virtually no public contact. There was minimal chit chat—a few whispers now and then, but that was the extent of it. The work day was carefully structured; everyone went to lunch at exactly 11:30, returned at exactly 12:15, and took a fifteen minute break at exactly 3:00. The opportunity to listen to music was a welcome relief. The work was monotonous, but the productivity rate was extremely high.

Mind Your Own Business

Concentrate on your own work and keep in mind that this is not a permanent job. Even if you feel that you are doing a grungy, insignificant little job that is boring and not the least bit glamorous, do it well. You are a temporary, which means that you will be moving on. Try to feel good about being productive and earning a paycheck. Someone just might notice how well you do that grungy little job and how nice you are to have around. And you may be surprised by a job offer that isn't grungy at all. It happens every day.

Don't be a braggart, a show-off, a leech, or a pesky motor-mouth. If you can help out with some useful information, fine. But it is not a good idea to go on and on about all the great jobs that you have had (permanent or temporary).

Office Rules

Follow the office routine and observe any rules and regulations. At times you will wonder why they instituted such a strange policy. And maybe it is a stupid waste of time and money. Or maybe you know of a place that has a better way of handling things. My advice: Zip it. You are on their turf now. It is hard for me to think of a policy that a temporary could justifiably raise objection to.

Usually the rules they ask you to follow are uniformly applied to all employees. Many offices have elaborate security procedures. Security cards and special entrance codes have become more common, but the offices have their reasons, and you are expected to follow the rules.

Other rules might concern eating and drinking at the desk, reading magazines and newspapers, smoking, and break times. You are completely out of line if you complain about or try to change company policy while filling a temporary assignment.

Handling Confidential Matters

I find that most employers are justifiably particular about the type of person they permit to have access to confidential material (personnel records, information about salaries, credit reports, correspondence to and from famous or influential people, etc.). They will often emphasize to the temporary help service and again to the temporary employee that the material is confidential. I am always flattered to be considered for such assignments. You should be, too. It shows that the service and the client trust you. Such assignments are not filled haphazardly.

Don't be concerned or offended if you are required to work on certain projects in an isolated atmosphere. It has happened to me several times. I was put in a room, and instructed not to talk to anyone other than the executive for whom I was working. The material was indeed extremely confidential. It was clear to me why she preferred to have someone working on it who had no vested interest in or close ties with anyone in the company.

Productivity

It is unacceptable for you to be less productive and efficient than the regular employees or previous temps. It is not enough for you to be as good as the other workers. You must be better; you must be more polite, more conscientious, more discreet, and more industrious. You must be more everything.

Be polite, be professional, work hard, and do the best that you can. And always bring along a sense of humor. You may not always have the opportunity to use it, but bring it along with you anyway. Let it be your secret. It will get you through some difficult times, and you will be surprised at how much you will be appreciated even in the stodgiest, stuffiest atmosphere.

If you leave a trail for the permanent (returning) employee, there is an excellent chance you will be asked for by name when they need someone again.

Unusually Pleasant Assignments

If you have an unusually pleasant experience at an assignment, let the service know, and take the time to write a brief thank-you note to the employer. Your résumé shouldn't accompany the note. Just say "Thanks" if the experience was a special one. I have done this several times. It is indeed a small world, and I recently received a call from a supervisor I hadn't seen since I worked for her on a temporary assignment seven years ago. She needed me to do some freelance work and she preferred to deal with me directly.

Also, thank those responsible at your service. Drop a note to your assignment coordinator, or attach a note to your time card: "Judy, this was a wonderful assignment. Thanks."

Go the Extra Mile

During the last few days of job assignments that have had a few rough spots, I have often gone beyond the call of duty and worked extra hard to make life a bit easier for all concerned. Try this sometime. Let's say the work load was heavy (but you handled it like a Super Temp), a few people were not so nice (and you also handled them). But you are moving on. It is often better to put forth a really Herculean effort those last few days; smile and be nice to everyone, come in a little early, skip a few breaks, offer to do a little more than you are asked to do.

You might surprise yourself. You may find that during the last few days your attitude about that job will change. Instead of thinking: "Thank goodness I am getting out of this place," you might be thinking: "Well, this hasn't really been all that bad. I did a good job. It's time to say farewell and move on." Then do just that. It really won't kill you to be nice to everyone for a day even if they don't reciprocate.

View Each Job as a Learning Experience

Every job assignment has been a learning experience in one form or another. Either I learned something about a particular industry, a new procedure, a better way of doing something, or I learned some things about human nature.

Temporary Status

Never, ever, refer to yourself as "just a temporary." Not even jokingly. Don't use your temporary status as an excuse for incompetence, laziness, lack of direction in your life, or anything else, and never apologize for it. If you refer to yourself as "just a temporary" or "only an insignificant someone who is passing through," you will be treated as exactly that —an insignificant someone. Perhaps more importantly, you will set the stage for the next temporary to be treated that way as well.

If you act like "Super Temp," the chances are greater that you will be treated like the pro you know you are instead of "just another temp."

Consider this: although the client is in the catbird seat, you wield a considerable amount of power. You represent yourself and your service. I always felt that it was gratifying to walk into a difficult situation and save the day—being a "Super Temp" requires considerable expertise, flexibility, diplomacy, and tenacity. Don't underestimate yourself.

Goodwill

If the first few days go well, take some candy and a dish (or a pretty flower) to the office to share with others. This promotes goodwill and is a very nice gesture. People really appreciate it.

Don't Move In

Don't take photographs of your spouse, lover, children, pets, or other personal items with you on a temporary assignment, even if the assignment is long term. If the assignment turns into a permanent job, then you can "settle in." But bringing anything other than tissues and hand lotion to a temporary assignment sends the message: "I am counting on being around for a long time." Don't count on anything, even if someone in authority has praised you and encouraged you to apply and interview for a permanent job. If things work out and the temporary job becomes a permanent job, fine— move in. Otherwise, move on.

Also, once an assignment is over, it is over. Maybe you will be called back, but probably not. *Do not* go back and "hang out" at the place where you just completed a job assignment. This is simply bad form. This is especially important if you have not found another job, temporary or permanent. Oh, sure, everyone will be nice and polite, but despite the smiles on their faces and yours, even if you really were "just in the neighborhood," stay away.

It is especially tacky to bring your adorable toddlers in, to ask to use their copy machine to make copies of your résumé, and to bemoan the fact that you don't have another assignment. I actually know of an instance where this happened. I was one of two temporaries hired by the same firm. The other was let go and the client retained me for a while longer. The other temporary apparently felt she had bonded with some of the permanent employees, and she periodically came in to "say, 'Hi!'" and spent an hour or so wandering around the office talking to everyone. In addition, she called frequently and told anyone who would listen about her marital problems. Not exactly a class act. Of course, as soon as she walked out the door or hung up the phone, the permanent employees used her as fodder for the office grapevine.

When you are between assignments, your job is to find another one. Intensify your efforts to get work. While you are "hanging out," your service may be trying to reach you. Get on with your life. Much later, if you are settled into an other assignment or a permanent job, it's OK to go back and say hello to some of the great folks you have worked for. If they were truly nice people they will be happy that you are doing well. Just don't overdo it.

GO PREPARED

If your car needs gas, get it the day before.

Stop for a moment just before leaving your house. Do you have everything? Glasses? Contact lens solution? Hand lotion? Aspirin, throat lozenges, prescription medication? Tissues or handkerchief? Time card? Directions? Phone number of your service?

What to Take

Make sure you take a few blank time cards with you.

Always bring your own note pad and pen to take notes. Sometimes these things will be provided, but it is still a good idea to have a few of your own. Write down names, descriptions, diagrams, phone extensions— anything that will help you do your job.

It also makes sense to make short notes to aid you in recognition of faces and names. For example, you might want to scribble a brief description of certain people, especially if there are several Jims or Lauras. However, I don't suggest writing down descriptions that might be considered offensive or unprofessional. You don't want to describe anyone as "the battle axe with the orthopedic shoes" or "the sexy hunk in the Armani suit with hair begging to be touched." Ahem. Either keep your descriptions appropriate or code them for your understanding only.

Make sure you have money for parking and transportation, lunch, snacks, etc. Take extra change— especially quarters for pay telephones and vending machines; coin changers don't always work. Don't ever borrow money from people at the job site.

What's that? You say you're broke? Then do what I've done on a few occasions: Fix yourself a nice breakfast, take an apple, drive to the parking lot of a shopping center and eat it in your car while reading a magazine or listening to the radio. I promise that you won't die of starvation. Better yet, take a walk while eating that apple. There is nothing pathetic or shameful about this. If you are working in the downtown area of a city, you will cross paths with other walkers and joggers.

Do's and Don'ts

Don't mooch. That applies not only to money, but also to stamps, chewing gum, cigarettes, cosmetics, etc.

Women: keep a new pair of hose in your purse or tote bag in the event of a snag or run.

Watch your purse, wallet, tote bag, or briefcase, etc., very carefully. *You* are responsible for it. If it is not possible to lock it up, then take it with you when you leave your work area, even if you are told it's OK to leave it. I have an even better suggestion regarding valuables: don't carry your driver's license, credit cards, and checkbook with blank checks into the office unless it is absolutely necessary. Hide those items from sight and lock them in your car, or leave them at home. It is also a good idea not to carry more cash than you need for the day.

I speak from experience. I had my wallet stolen from my purse by an intruder while I was on a temporary job assignment. The purse was in my desk drawer. I left the desk for less than a minute. The thief, who is still at large as of this writing, had a virtual field day with my driver's license, credit cards, and especially my checkbook. This caused me some major hassles and headaches. I had to take time off to call the police, bank, and credit card companies.

Beware of "office creepers." Protect yourself and your possessions at all times.

Prepare your clothes the night before. Prepare several ensembles. This is insurance against popped buttons, ripped seams, broken zippers, makeup smudges, clinging children with jelly on their fingers, and coffee spills.

Don't ask if it is OK to smoke. It probably isn't. If it is permitted, you will notice soon enough. Even if you are encouraged to "feel free" to smoke at your desk, don't do so the first morning. You will have your hands full enough learning about and doing your job.

Lunch

Even if your temporary service tells you it's OK to brown bag, be aware that some office workers can be very territorial about their kitchens and their appliances, and they don't like the idea of a stranger using their microwave to heat up last week's cabbage or taking up space in their refrigerator, especially on the first day of the job assignment. Be aware of this and be courteous enough to ask if there is a policy regarding these items. I've found it helpful to bring something on the first day which doesn't require refrigeration or heating.

Wait for your supervisor to tell you the procedure regarding lunch and coffee break(s). If you are not told, you will have to ask—later in the day. But wait for an appropriate amount of time to pass. It shouldn't be, or appear to be, your top priority.

WHAT TO EXPECT—SOME TYPICAL ASSIGNMENTS

OK, now that you know some do's and don'ts, let's go over the whole process from start to finish with some examples from my experience. I'll start with the "typical" and move to the unexpected—but possible—from there.

Some Typical Assignments

Both of these qualify as examples of the "normal," average temporary assignment.

Once, the temporary service called me on a Monday morning and told me they had a client needing someone to fill in for a week for a secretary who would be off for about three or four weeks recuperating from surgery. The office had tried to get along without her, but it was overloading the other secretaries. The assignment involved answering telephones, typing, sorting mail, and doing some relatively simple filing tasks.

I was given the "specs" (specifications):

- Name of the client
- Location (street address, floor number)
- Working hours (8:00 to 4:45 with an hour for lunch)
- The name of the person to report to
- The pay rate I would receive for this assignment
- Information about the office atmosphere

I accepted the assignment and reported to work that afternoon. The office was a small unit of a larger government agency. There were three other secretaries, in addition to the one I was filling in for, and twelve professional staff members.

Upon arrival (I got there early), I was offered a cup of coffee and waited a few minutes for my supervisor to arrive. I was introduced to everyone, shown how to answer the phones, taken to the copy center, the mail room, the rest room, and the lunch room. My supervisor stayed with me for a while to oversee telephone calls and mail sorting. When she felt comfortable about leaving me on my own, she went to do her own work. It was all pretty standard.

I plunged in and did what needed to be done. Everyone was congenial, and they were willing to answer questions. I made myself a map of the office and a list of names (first and last) and areas of responsibility. I was given a weekly schedule indicating which staff members would be in or out of the office on various dates (they traveled a lot). This list also contained telephone numbers where people could be reached when they were out of the office. This was very helpful. Staff also called in regularly for messages.

I had a problem with the copy machine one day, but I found someone to help me, and it was no big deal. During the second week of the assignment, the staff threw a big party (at another location) for their boss. I was in the office alone for a few hours, but it was not a problem.

The work was routine, the personalities were all very different, but they seemed to blend well together. One woman was a computer enthusiast and we worked exceptionally well together.

I made the mistake of teasing one man I didn't know very well, and his reaction showed me that he really preferred not to be teased, so I respected that. But he was a nice man. Some staff members made a few remarks about other staff members, but I just smiled without making any comments one way or the other.

The assignment went by without incident and ended after three weeks. On Wednesday of the third week, I was told that the regular secretary was going to return to work the following Monday. I called my coordinator to let her know. On Friday, she lined up another assignment for me. Before leaving, I said goodbye to everyone, and they thanked me for my help.

On another occasion, I was asked to report to a law firm to fill in for a couple of days for a secretary who was ill. I was pleased to accept the assignment because I had worked there six months previously, and I remembered that the assignment had gone well.

The first day I wasn't very busy— several people were out of the office, and one of the attorneys was returning from vacation. I answered the phones, did some copying, and made revisions to material that the permanent secretary had already stored on disk. The second and third days were very busy. I transcribed tapes from Dictaphone, and most of the documents were lengthy. The offices were lavish, and the people were courteous. Coffee and snacks were provided free of charge. There was no time for chatter, which was fine. I wasn't there to socialize; I was sent to do a job. The decor, furniture, and equipment (computers, copy machine, telephones) were definitely state of the art.

I did what had to be done, asked questions when I needed to, and kept busy. My only problem was in finding a lengthy document which required revisions. I was told that it was stored on disk, but could not find it. Two other secretaries helped me search for it, but the document was never found. The other secretary helped me to retype the document.

On the last day, they thanked me, signed my time card, and I left. Mission accomplished.

These were neither "plum" nor "prune" assignments. They were typical of most of the assignments I have had.

EXPECT THE UNEXPECTED

Be aware that not all assignments are typical. Some are terrible and some are just plain bizarre. As I look at the log I have kept of the many different job assignments I have worked on, several things occur to me. Some of the jobs were absolutely, positively terrific (better than any permanent job I have had, at any level). Others were lousy. A few were truly horrible. Most were OK. But if I were to pick the best, the worst, and the one that gets the prize — hands down — for being the craziest and most bizarre, I know exactly which ones they would be.

The following examples from my own experience are extreme — most jobs are not on such extreme ends of the spectrum, but somewhere in between, as illustrated above. But the exceptions are out there and you should know about them.

The Best—Hotel Heaven

I have had many wonderful temporary job assignments. But there is no question about which one was my favorite.

My coordinator had just received a job order for an Executive Secretary to the General Manager of a hotel. His secretary had been terminated, and I was forewarned that I would be walking into a difficult situation. I braced myself for difficulty, but it was great. I enjoyed the work and the atmosphere tremendously. On top of this, the job had lots of perks which, as a temporary, I didn't expect. One of these was free meals in the hotel restaurant; great meals — not just soup, sandwiches, and chips. (I gained eight pounds that I didn't want or need.)

My supervisor, the General Manager, was a dynamic, extremely hard working, ultra professional executive. His standards were high and he had recently been transferred to the job from another city. He had a hotel to run, personnel problems to deal with, and he had recently had to fire his secretary. It was amazing to be around him and watch him in action. He was the epitome of the "high powered, driven executive," somewhat intimidating, but a wonderful manager.

He noticed the efforts I made to "go the extra mile," and took time to tell me how much he appreciated it. He caught some other staff members trying to slip me some of their work, and nipped it in the bud. Fast. This man was the type of executive who only had to admonish people once. They did not want an encore. Although he was a tough taskmaster, his style made you want to do a good job.

The workload was heavy, and the job of Executive Secretary was high pressure. I was helping on a special project, which involved a lot of confidential typing, copying, and collating. In addition, I was having personal difficulties. I had been laid off from a permanent job and had just moved out of the apartment that I had been able to afford and had lived in for six years because I couldn't keep up the rent. My car had conked out several times. My support system was waning and my self esteem was dangerously close to zero. But I still managed to get cleaned up, go to work every day, be cheerful, and do the best work that I possibly could.

One day, it got to be too much. The pressure became intense, tempers were short, and I became confused about something I was working on. I had to ask the General Manager (twice) to explain a few things, and he went over it with me (twice). I became frustrated and upset. I was trying as hard as I could. For a couple of minutes I just sat there and considered getting my purse, walking out of the hotel, and driving as far away as the three dollars worth of gas in my tank would take me. Soon I got a grip on the situation, and plunged in. But I was still confused about one task.

The Food and Beverage Manager was also involved in the project that I was working on. She stopped by to see how it was coming. I told her that I was confused, but that I did not feel comfortable asking the manager for instructions a third time. She tried to clarify things and left me to do my work.

About ten minutes later, the General Manager came in. He told me that I was doing a terrific job, and asked me if I had any questions. I asked for the clarification that I needed. He patiently explained the task, and I finally understood it. Then he sat down with me and literally rolled up his sleeves, and helped me for about a half hour: sorting, proofreading, stapling, etc. Several staff members came in to try to talk to him, but he made them wait.

After I finished the project, I went back to my desk and worked on some other things. That same day, I received a call offering me a permanent job that I had applied for and interviewed for several months earlier. It was a good job, and I accepted.

I was to start my new job in two weeks, which was fine because it coincided with the end of the temp assignment at the hotel. The General Manager had already made arrangements to hire as permanent replacement a secretary who had worked for him before, but who was not immediately available.

During the last few days of that assignment, I really felt sad. I was anxious to start a permanent job and get my life back to normal, but I had really loved working at the hotel.

On my last day at the hotel, I was given a surprise farewell party, complete with a huge cake personally designed by the chef. It was really something. There were lots of tears and hugs and good wishes.

About four years later, through a series of coincidences, I had the pleasure of talking to the man who had been the hotel manager. He had moved to another state, and was doing extremely well. He has since become a virtual celebrity in the hotel industry. I continue to hear good things about him.

The Worst—Time Card Torture

I was sent to be a "clerk typist" in the mortgage loan department of a company. The work was actually that of a mortgage loan processor, but the client called in a job order for a clerk typist.

I am not sure why, but the woman who was my supervisor behaved as though her goal was to make life miserable for the temporaries in general, and me in particular. She screamed at me in front of people, loaded me up with tasks, imposed impossible deadlines, and was generally a really nasty person.

She began each day with a loud sugary, "Good Morning!" and a false grin. Then she began her various games, and she had quite a repertoire.

After putting up with her for two weeks, I complained to the service. They asked me if I could finish the assignment (it was scheduled to end in another two weeks), and I agreed to try to stick it out. That was a mistake.

Her favorite game was Time Card Torture. Let me tell you how it worked.

My work hours were 8:00 A.M. to 5:00 P.M. My lunch break began at 11:00 A.M., which was a little early, but at least I got a lunch break. I was always on time — usually early. I worked hard, and I was much nicer to this woman than she merited.

On Friday at about 4:30 in the afternoon, I took my time card in to her and said I would pick it up later. She put her hands on her hips and said, "I can't sign it yet." At 5:00 she was nowhere to be found. I finally located her in the break room making quite a show of putting her feet up on the table and reading a magazine. She scrutinized the time card unnecessarily, told me to follow her back to her office where she made a big production of adding up the hours—several times —on her calculator! I had worked a standard forty-hour work week. It doesn't take high level math to calculate eight hours a day times five. Then she sighed, looked at her wristwatch, and signed it. As I attempted to take it, she grasped it tightly and said, "I'd like for you to work harder next week."

This exact same scene replayed each week, and I informed my service about it each time. I also relayed other inappropriate behavior on the part of this supervisor. My coordinator called her and asked if she was having a problem understanding time card procedures. She said "No," and told my coordinator that she felt I was doing a good job. But her odd behavior towards me continued.

One day, at exactly 11:00 A.M., the beginning of my designated lunch time, she came to me with a puzzled look on her face. She said she was having trouble finding the telephone number of a hair salon, and she asked me to call information. I did. Without thanking me, she loudly exclaimed that she felt I wasn't working fast enough. I responded that if she was not satisfied with my performance, she should get someone else — a replacement. She didn't respond verbally. Instead, she brought out a stack of work and emphasized that it had to be completed and ready for her boss's signature by 1:00 p.m. I knew that this was true because I had heard her boss discussing the documents earlier in the day.

I chose to leave the work there and take my lunch as scheduled. While eating lunch, I reached the decision that I was not going back. Her behavior had gotten progressively out of hand. I called the service and reiterated the problems on the job assignment. I told them I was not going back. This was not their preference, but they seemed to understand ultimately and lined up another job assignment for me which started the very next day.

Sometimes, no matter how hard you work or how hard you try to get along with those around you, you will run into someone beyond reason. It is best to try to work it out with your service in advance, but it is not appropriate for them to expect you to stay in a situation which is unprofessional and unhealthy. Only you can determine where the breaking point is for you in any particular situation. Just be aware that strange people are out there in the business world and you must take care of yourself.

The Craziest—If it Sounds too Good...

One Monday morning about a week before Christmas, having finished a long-term assignment as a legal secretary, I was preparing to enjoy a couple of days respite before beginning another job assignment. At about 9:30 A.M. I received a call from my service asking if I was interested in filling up the holes (i.e., taking on a short assignment prior to starting another longer one). I said, "Sure, tell me about it." My coordinator told me that the job consisted of typing proposals at the client's home in a suburb of Columbus, using a laptop computer and WordPerfect 5.1 software. The pay rate was very good; comparable to that of a legal secretary.

I said that I was interested, but that I would prefer to do the work at home on my own computer since I had Word-Perfect 5.1. I was given the telephone number of a woman coordinating the work for the client, I'll call her Sandy. I spoke with Sandy. She told me that the client was a man I will call "Artie." She explained that the job was to come to her house, work for a while on a regular computer, then take a portable laptop over to Artie's house to work for a couple of days. After discussing the possibility of me working from my own computer at home, Sandy told me that Artie said he didn't care what computer I used or where I worked from, as long as the work was done. So I drove over to Sandy's house to get the material, and arrived at 12:00 noon.

Sandy explained that she was waiting for Artie to send over some material via a local messenger/courier service, and she had some material for me to work on while we were waiting. (The time spent at her house was the most pleasant part of the assignment.)

I noticed that there were several calls back and forth between Sandy and Artie. She seemed exasperated with him, and indicated to me that she wasn't going to be spending much more time on the project.

It was agreed that I would work from my home, and that material would be delivered and picked up by messenger service, and that I would be paid for any time "on call" — making myself available and waiting for work. I explained that I was willing to put in eight to ten hours per day over the course of the next three days, but I would have to shut down at 10:00 P.M. Wednesday because I had to start another job assignment on Thursday.

At about 4:00 P.M. the material arrived, and I took it home to begin working. I called the temporary help service and explained the nature of the assignment, that I was working from home, and that I was charging for time spent "on call." The service had no problem with that.

As I began working, I thought to myself: "This is great. The work isn't bad, the pay is good, I can work at home in my sweats, or my bathrobe, the work will be picked up and delivered at the client's expense, and no one is breathing down my neck." This was a nice change of pace assignment. Almost too good to be true.

For the remainder of the evening, I worked on the material that I had brought from Sandy's house, spent some time on phone calls to and from Sandy, and waited for the messenger service. Sandy told me that if no work was delivered by 10:00 P.M. to shut down, and she would call me in the morning. Artie did not send over any work that first night.

There were dozens of telephone calls back and forth between me and Artie over the next couple of days and nights. He apologized for sounding rushed or rude. He told me that I was doing a fine job, and he had figured out a system. He said that he was going to run a "shuttle service" with the messengers — from his house to mine. Artie seemed certain that things would now run more smoothly. He seemed exasperated at Sandy and others who had worked for him.

It was discovered that I had no master disk — a shell to use as a guideline that would save a lot of time retyping text which remained constant throughout several different proposals. Artie became more exasperated. He said he would send the messenger over with a master disk right away.

About an hour later, the messenger arrived. While I was working on the material, Artie called and gave me more instructions. I had to call him several times for clarification on his writing. For example, there were some unfinished sentences, and his writing and grammar skills were not good.

When I was almost finished, I called and told Artie to

send the messenger. I mentioned to him that I had some blank disks and a copy of a sample proposal that belonged to him. He told me to keep the material since I had agreed to work the next evening (Thursday).

On Thursday I started a different job assignment at a law firm. When I got home from work at about 6:00 P.M., I noticed that Artie had not left any messages. The agreement was that I would go "on the clock" at 7:00 P.M. So I fixed dinner, and waited for him to call. At 7:30, I still hadn't heard from Artie. I called him. He said that he was tired— he and his wife had been working all night, he had gone to the airport to send some material at 5:30 this morning, and he essentially told me to forget it for tonight. He asked if I could work that weekend, and I said that I could put in some time on Sunday if necessary. He said he would call me on Sunday. So I relaxed and prepared to go shopping. About fifteen minutes later, as I was dressing, the phone rang. It was Artie. He asked if I would come over to his house to work. I declined—politely.

About five minutes later Artie called again. He sounded like a completely different person. He wanted a breakdown of how many hours I had worked on which project and how much time I had spent waiting around. (What happened to "Karen, babe, you're a lifesaver, and a wonderful human being?") What a turnaround. After some discussion, we agreed that I would deduct five hours from my time card since I wasn't working that evening. He wanted to know the billing rate and my pay rate. I told him he would have to discuss that with the service, that those details had been clarified when Sandy called in the job order. Artie said: "Well, Sandy has this stuff so screwed up, and I am just trying to straighten things out." I asked him if he had a problem with the number of hours I was charging since we had discussed it in advance. He said: "No, I don't have a problem with anything you have done."

Later that evening, it became clear to me that I didn't want to work for Artie that Sunday or at any other time. It was too much hassle. I had fulfilled the three-day commitment (which turned into four days). Enough was enough. The next day, I called the service and told them about the recent phone calls from Artie.

A few days later I stopped in the office of my service to attend the Christmas party, pick up my paycheck, and drop off a "package." I had composed a letter explaining that I was deducting five hours from my time card, and I enclosed the blank disks and Artie's sample proposal. The letter said simply, "Mr. _____ should make arrangements to pick up this material, either personally or by messenger service, from your offices, during regular business hours."

Apparently Artie had gone through several temps over the course of the past few days. Several other staff members at the temporary help service told me that Artie had called and complained about every temporary — including me. It is interesting that although Artie kept complaining about the temps, he kept putting in job orders. Most clients would have gone to another service if in fact they were that dissatisfied.

As the Christmas festivities got underway, another temporary employee walked in. It turns out that she had worked at Artie's house on the previous day. She was virtually in tears. Apparently the agreement had been for her to work from 9:00 A.M. until 4:30 P.M., but he had convinced her to stay until 7:30 P.M. She said she was upset because she was supposed to pick up her dead father's ashes.

Another temp who had actually quit on him after working at his house was in another room preparing documentation about the situation. The vice president of the temporary help service added that Artie had called her at home late the previous night, ranting and raving. Just another one of those things that can happen on temporary assignments.

RANKING THE INDUSTRIES

Now that we have looked at specific incidents, I would like to talk in generalizations about industries. Having worked for so many different companies and industries, I feel that I am in a position to draw certain conclusions. My opinions are based on facts and actual experiences, a lot of different experiences.

While it would be inaccurate and unfair to form an opinion based on a few isolated experiences (good or bad), that is not the case. Certain types of organizations and industries display certain propensities, and trends with regard to management styles, working styles, personalities, and atmosphere. I have included the information I feel most useful to you.

The Most Pleasant Industries

HOSPITALITY. This includes hotels, lodges, resorts, hospitals, and retirement communities. I am referring to the administrative arm of the industry. The very nature of the hospitality industry is accommodating. I have spoken to people who have various levels of jobs in the hospitality industry, and while there were exceptions, most of them seem to agree with this assessment.

LAW FIRMS. Does this choice surprise you? Let me explain what I like about interacting with law firms and attorneys. The work is usually interesting, often exciting. The offices are usually very well run and organized. In fact, law firms get my vote for most efficient and best organized industry.

I have been fortunate enough to have considerable contact, as both an employee and a client, with many successful firms. Highly educated people and aesthetically pleasing offices impress me.

I have been required to work very hard, but have enjoyed the work and have usually been treated very well by law firms. In addition, some of the perks are fabulous.

The Least Pleasant Industries

FINANCE. This includes banks, investment firms, mortgage companies. Why? I found the atmosphere to be very robotic and intense. High pressure? Yes, but that is common in many other industries, and that—in and of itself—really doesn't bother me. It was something more than pressure. It can best be described as a nervous energy colored by insecurity, suspicion, and hidden agendas.

These organizations also tended to "crack the whip" — whether or not it was necessary. They monitored temporaries much more closely than other types of organizations. There were several instances when supervisors came to me and other temporaries and made sure that we had enough to do, even when it was obvious that we had more than enough work for the rest of the day.

In addition, there are no perks to speak of. People in general seem to go overboard to show that they are busy. Turnover and dissension among permanent employees seem to be unusually high, particularly among the lower ranks.

Most Diverse

GOVERNMENT AGENCIES. Having worked for many years in permanent jobs with government agencies, this diversity was no surprise. My experiences on temporary assignments reinforced my beliefs. It is a mistake to form stereotypical ideas about employees, workload, or working atmosphere in the government. Some offices are fast paced and high pressure. Others are extremely laid back, and a few even have a folksy, homespun style. Equally diverse are the people who work in government agencies—the bureaucrats.

Some are of the highest caliber and very pleasant to work with; some are very hardworking; others are zombies just putting in their time and bumping into walls; and you might run into some real crazies. In that sense, the government— city, county, state, or federal— is no different from the private sector.

Most Attractive People (Male and Female)

In my experience, the most attractive people are found in banks, investment companies, and law firms. This is an added bonus in the law firms and investment companies, and a pleasant surprise in banks.

Biggest Surprise—Worst Goof-offs

Contrary to popular belief, the worst goof-offs are *not* in government offices. They are in the private sector. To make matters even worse, the private sector supervisors are more brazen about it. They have no shame whatsoever about dumping work on a temporary while their permanent employees come in late, take long lunches, read magazines, take and make personal calls, stand around gossiping, and knock off early. Often the powers that be condone this nonsense; some even seem to encourage it. Don't ask me why— I can't figure it out.

There are goof-offs in the public sector, but they tend to be more clever about it. They will make a perfunctory effort to look busy and hide their newspapers and magazines. Not so in the private sector. They are bold. It seems as though they actually want the temporary employee(s) to see that they are not working. They almost dare you to complain or object.

Before anyone gets offended or takes issue, please remember—it is important to consider your own personal preferences and style. My "most" may be your "least." Or what you consider to be the "best" or "worst" may be types of businesses and industries that didn't make any of my lists.

6

Problems with the Temporary Help Service

Your temporary help companies and especially your assignment coordinators can be your best allies. It is not only important, it is essential to establish and maintain a good rapport. If you have good chemistry with them, life can be so much easier, especially during the tough times.

Even so, there will likely be problems. Some of the more common ones follow.

NO JOBS

The very nature of the temporary services business is erratic. Sometimes there just are not enough job assignments to keep everyone busy. Temporary help companies face the task of matching individual worker skills with specific client needs.

For example, there may be five workers waiting to be sent on long-term executive secretarial assignments, but the only unfilled job order is a three-day assignment for two file clerks and it is in an area of town in which you have indicated you prefer not to work.

Or maybe you want secretarial jobs but you don't have good telephone expertise. Perhaps a client company needs, and is willing to pay very handsomely for, several people with at least two years of experience in collecting delinquent corporate accounts. You are willing to learn, but the client does not want to have to train you. This is not the fault of the temporary help service.

It can be frustrating to respond to a recruitment ad from a temporary help company, and then be told by that very same company that there is no work for you. It is possible that you are getting the runaround, or that assignments are being given to someone's friend of a friend. Don't wait too long for a service to put you to work. If you are treated shabbily by a temporary help company, or if they can't keep you busy, it might help at least to make an effort to talk to the manager about it. If nothing is resolved, perhaps a written complaint will help. You might get some mental satisfaction ("I guess I told *them*!") But don't expect miracles. Most importantly, don't waste valuable time on a hopeless crusade or vendetta. Simply register with other services.

General economic conditions play an important role in the temporary help industry. I had no problem getting steady job assignments in 1985. That year I temped for seven straight months with no down time whatsoever. Some of the assignments were better than others, but I had steady work. Then I stopped doing temporary assignment work and accepted a permanent job that I had found on my own. Four years later, I got back into temporary assignment work.

But beginning in the summer of 1990, especially after the Persian Gulf crisis, I ran into lots of gaps, even though I was registered with several temporary help services. Job assignments were short term and sporadic. Economic realities prevented companies from automatically calling in job orders for a temporary. There was another lull during the summer of 1991. However, this one had a different dynamic. Many companies "jumped the gun"—they called in job orders, confirmed the arrangements, and then canceled the job orders at the last minute. This is extremely frustrating for temporary help companies and temporary employees. There is more about this in Chapter 9.

In many cases during both lulls, employers were forced to make do with the staff they had. Even when they did use temporary employees, they contracted them for shorter periods of time. As I was told by one temporary help company with offices nationwide, "We are noticing a sharp drop in clientele. We are having to concentrate more on drumming up business and we are making concessions to clients (lowering rates, etc.) in some instances. Clients are cutting back until the economy gets better. They are viewing temporary employees as excess baggage except in unusual cases. We have even had to cut back on benefits offered to our temporary employees (holiday and vacation pay after working a certain number of hours, etc.)."

In addition, many employees who were laid off during

this period still needed to earn a living. Many of them registered with temporary services, increasing the competition for the available jobs. In Chapter 3, I outlined various reasons people choose to work as temporary employees. One of the most obvious reasons is survival.

During these periods, the jobs I refer to as "plum" assignments were few and far between, and I found myself accepting more standard assignments such as file clerk, data entry operator, and receptionist. The assignment lengths were often for only a few days instead of weeks or months with the exception of maternity leaves. These assignments usually lasted from six weeks to several months. Recession or no recession, women still need to take time off to have babies. Even so, things didn't really pick up again until the fall of 1991.

What You Can Do

When things are slow and even when they pick up, there are things you can do to assist yourself. Several factors contributed to my finding the steady work assignments I had in late 1991 and on into 1992:

PERSISTENCE. I did not sit home and wait for the phone to ring. I consistently let services know that I wanted and needed work.

RAPPORT. My rapport with two particular temporary help companies was excellent. They knew that when an assignment was coming to an end I would want another one, unless I told them otherwise.

SKILLS AND EXPERIENCE. I am convinced that if I did not have computer skills in addition to many years of solid work experience in various industries, I would have had to settle for less desirable assignments or worse—no work at all.

THE WRONG JOBS

Sometimes, jobs or aspects of jobs are misrepresented by the client firm or misunderstood by the service. Be specific and firm about the length and types of assignments you want. If you are a dynamite word processor, but you hate answering phones, let them know. If you only want to work for law firms or medical offices, say so. Speak up. Some temporary help services specialize; i.e., they only hire accounting personnel, legal secretaries, medical transcribers, etc.

Be careful about saying you are willing to do anything, no matter how desperate you might be, unless you truly are willing to do anything. If there are certain companies or industries for whom you do not want to work, tell your service. It is a small world, and don't be surprised if you are offered an assignment at the offices of a former employer. Do you really want to go back to work as a temporary in an office from which you resigned or were "let go"? Maybe, but probably not.

Also, consider logistics and the location of the job assignments. If you do not have a reliable car, tell the coordinator that you can only take assignments that are accessible via public transportation. You don't want to spend your paychecks on taxis or have to rely on a friend to get you to and from work! In addition, unless I know exactly where I am supposed to go to work, I always try to drive by the location the night before. This may sound like a bit much, but it can save you, the client company, and your service lots of aggravation and embarrassment. There is more on this in Chapter 7.

THE RUNAROUND

Unfortunately, this also happens. There are some temporary help companies that don't treat their employees very well. Some coordinators will string temporary employees along, or simply lie to them and to client companies, in order to earn a commission. If you have a really bad experience, and you feel that the temporary help service was at fault and/or treated you unfairly, you can send a written complaint to the CEO of the company and also to your local Better Business Bureau. Calling and writing and documenting take time, and there is always a lot of back and forth "he said/she said/they said/that's not what I was told ... " rhetoric. Don't waste too much time with these people. It really isn't worth it. You can, and should, move on. Quickly. (See Chapter 3 for more ways to deal with the disadvantages of doing temporary assignment work.)

I had three experiences with temporary services that enraged and upset me so much that I decided to follow up by doing something about it. In one case I wrote a letter to the President of the company, in another instance I wrote to the Better Business Bureau, and in the other I called and spoke with the manager, who asked me to put my concerns in writing. I received responses from all three. Generally speaking, all concerned were courteous. Two were apologetic, but they went on to explain their side of the story and what they felt was justification for their actions. One temporary help company lied — plain and simple. The fact that the situations were looked into and that my complaints were addressed did make me feel better. But all three experiences left a very bad taste in my mouth. I never did business with these people again, nor did I recommend their services to anyone. Nothing was really resolved, perhaps because the nature of my complaints was not serious enough to merit any formal action.

I want to make it clear that I am not referring to cases of harassment, discrimination or unfair labor practices, etc. I am not an attorney, and no part of this book should be interpreted as legal advice. That is not my area of expertise. I am 100% behind anyone who truly feels she has a case and wants to pursue some type of recourse. This includes anyone who feels a victim of sexism, racism, age discrimination, sexual harassment, etc.

A COMMITMENT IS A COMMITMENT—OR IS IT?

Generally speaking, a temporary employee who accepts an assignment is expected to perform the specified duties for the period of time indicated when the job order is placed. In other words, if you accept a two-week job assignment as a clerk typist at XYZ Company, you are expected to stick with it for the duration.

Sometimes a temporary employee will decide to end the assignment for any one of various reasons: he is not treated well; the job is not what it was represented to be; another employer has offered her a permanent job; there has been serious illness or family emergency, etc. My experiences and those of other temporaries with whom I have talked indicate that most—but not all—temporary help companies are reasonable about assigning you elsewhere or releasing you if you have a good reason.

If you get offered a permanent job that you interviewed for a couple of weeks earlier, that has to be your top priority. I feel that you should give at least a few days' notice and help to organize things. Offer to train your replacement and leave on a positive note.

Problems sometimes arise regarding interpretation of the term "commitment," as it relates to the length of the assignment. This can usually be traced back to the client company ("We want someone for one week, maybe two...").

Example: A service once called and offered me a job assignment. They stated, "We have a client who wants someone for one week, maybe longer, full-time from 8:30 until

5:00, starting tomorrow." I accepted the assignment. A few minutes later I got a call from another service offering me an assignment for the same dates, and I turned it down, explaining that I was booked on those dates. A couple of hours later Service #1 called and said that the client had decided they only needed someone half days, from 8:30 until 12:30, for a week, possibly longer. Although I wasn't happy, I agreed to the part-time hours for a week. At the end of the week, the client still had not made up their mind as to whether they wanted my services part-time or full-time next week. I received an offer for a full-time assignment to begin the following week. I accepted. Service #1 was displeased. I pointed out that their client had initially placed the job order for forty hours a week, cut it down to twenty hours, and been vague about how long they would need me. I also explained to the coordinator that I had filled the assignment for a week, and had been told by the client that they didn't have enough work for me to do. But the coordinator still admonished me about commitments.

It is a fact that a double standard often exists in the temporary assignment market regarding honoring commitments. It is accepted if a client company calls in a job order, changes its mind at the last minute, and leaves the temporary employee hanging. (See Chapter 9.) But a temporary employee who ends an assignment, whatever the reason, risks an unfavorable response.

7

Problems with the Job Assignment

To one degree or another, all jobs, permanent and temporary, have their own sets of problems. In order to alleviate some of the problems and annoyances inherent in temporary assignment work, I find it best to try to be prepared for anything. The two qualities that are absolute essentials to success in any job assignment—permanent or temporary—are self-sufficiency and common sense. Make these two qualities your new best friends, they will serve you well.

This chapter will take you through several potential problem areas regarding temporary assignments. All of them present problems for some people, and most of them can be solved using common sense and self-sufficiency.

LOCATING THE JOB SITE AND NEARBY NECESSITIES

Make absolutely certain you know your way to and from the job site. Always double check the directions and suggestions of others in advance. If possible, drive to the job site the day before to make sure you know where you are going and how long it takes to get there. Never take a suggested shortcut or alternate route when you are on a time schedule. If you are told, "It's much faster to take Route 247 to the second exit—that's exit number 33B (or maybe it's 33C), then veer to the left for about three miles" ... or, "There is a great little sandwich shop just around the corner—it only takes a few seconds to get there and back..." Be skeptical.

I have been given some strange, supposedly "simple" directions by people who assured me that they knew their way around. In attempting to follow these directions, however, I wasted time and became lost. Was that their fault? Nope. It was mine. I should have listened, thanked them, and then either ignored their suggestions and taken the route which I was certain that I knew, or checked theirs out in advance.

It is not good enough to "know the general area." Make sure that you know how to get to the nearest bank, drugstore, sub shop, etc. Scope it out for yourself. It is no fun to spend your lunch hour (or drive home time) going on a scavenger hunt. If you take buses or use other modes of public transportation, make sure you know their schedules. Count on them being a little off schedule and plan accordingly.

ON SITE LOCATIONS

Listen carefully when instructions are given. If the company has no map, diagram, written instructions, or list of names and titles, make your own. When you finish the assignment, leave any helpful information for the person who is replacing you. If you have the time, you can actually put together an instruction folder for temporaries. (See Chapter 9.) I have done this several times, and clients always appreciate it. It is the type of task that few people have the foresight, time, knowledge, or desire to tackle.

DUTIES VARY FROM JOB ORDER

If the actual duties that you are asked to perform on the job assignment are different from those described to you by the service, call your coordinator. For example, some companies will request a receptionist to do light typing when what they really need is a secretary/word processor with experience working on spreadsheets and desktop publishing. The company is charged a lower fee rate for a receptionist/clerk typist than for a secretary or word processor.

Some employers are very slick about this and will attempt to justify the extra duties as "just a few short letters." Or they might ask to show you "a little bit" about their computer system because they "have some very simple data entry projects." The client company requested someone who did not necessarily have the skills to perform these duties. Now they want you, the temp, to give them more than their money was supposed to buy.

The client is not going to call the service and say, "What a great temporary employee! Please charge us more money because we are getting more than we are paying for and we don't want to take advantage of the temporary employee or the temporary help service." I do know of two instances where something close to that happened, but it is rare.

Some client companies will go to great lengths to structure a job so that it appears to consist of very basic clerical tasks, but actually the temp is performing the duties of a much higher level position. It is very important that you keep the client/service relationship honest. You must let the service know about this and insist on a pay adjustment, a work load adjustment, or another assignment. It is your responsibility to do so. On the other hand, you cannot expect top pay rates unless the duties of the job and your skills merit them. Don't complain to the client about being paid unfairly—that must be worked out with your service. If you can't work it out, move on as soon as possible, to a different assignment or another temporary service.

Some temporary services will really stand up for their temporaries and demand fair pay for the work required. For example: My favorite service had me lined up for a three-month assignment at a law firm. This was an important client. I had worked there before on a short assignment, and they asked for me by name. After things were finalized, the service received a call from the client, outlining budget woes, fiscal restrictions, and related problems. They wanted to know if the rate could be lowered. The service agreed to take a smaller cut of the total rate, but they also had their limitations. The client bristled and pressed for an even lower rate. My coordinator told them: "Look, you want a top notch temporary. You have specifically asked for Karen Mendenhall because you know her. We cannot and will not ask Karen to take a pay cut for this assignment. If you want a warm body that can just type fast, fine. I'll send you a puncher. But I can't send you a Karen for a lower rate of pay." The client relented. I know that this was all said because I happened to be standing in the office at the time.

TOO MUCH WORK TO DO

Many client companies make unreasonable demands on temporary employees. Forget about the fact you are doing more work than so and so, the permanent employee. That is an administrative problem within the client company and really is none of your business. I am referring to instances where you are expected to do more work than humanly possible within the time frame requested on a regular basis. If you are concerned that you cannot handle the unreasonable workload, your first step is to talk to your service about it. They should speak with the client. Don't be surprised if the client praises you. After all, you have been doing more work than should be expected of one person.

Often when a company has two or even more vacant positions, they will get one temporary to do the work of both full-time jobs. Maybe they have decided to "combine" the positions, but they rarely acknowledge the fact that one temp is knocking himself out doing two jobs (or trying to). It is possible, and in fact highly probable, that one temporary employee (no matter how efficient) will be unable to handle the workload to the satisfaction of the client company.

So, it's time for "the talk." The supervisor will call in the temporary. She will tread very carefully. If they have a good temporary employee, she won't want to mess up a good thing. Ignore the diplomatic phrasing, the message is, "We want you to work harder and faster."

This scene might replay itself a couple of times. It is not a reprimand — it is a polite "nudge." The client wants to get more out of one temporary because it is easier on the budget.

I have been in situations like this a few times. What did I do? First, I made the temporary help company aware of the tremendous workload and "the talk." Sometimes the temp service knew that the client was using one temp to fill one and a half, two, or even three vacant slots. Sometimes the service had no idea.

Once you inform the service of the situation, decide your action. If the job assignment is tolerable, stick with it. But sometimes management will push relentlessly. If they push too far and upset you, talk with your supervisor at the job site. Always try to do it privately, but sometimes that isn't possible. No matter how frustrated you are and how much you want to show it, breathe deeply, maintain your calmness, and say something like:

Gee, I'm confused. I feel that I am doing a good job. I am doing all I can. I am giving you 110% — my best. I'm efficient, punctual, I get along with everyone, and I don't goof off. You have told my service that I am doing a great job. But you expressed displeasure to me. I am willing to continue the assignment, but if you are dissatisfied with my performance, you should terminate me immediately and get someone else or perhaps do without, and I will simply move on.

It is important to curb your desire to exchange harsh words. Do not criticize their operations or other staff members. Do not remind them that you are filling two slots. Trust me, they already know this. If the client was truly dissatisfied with any aspect of your performance, you would have been out the door a long time ago.

Remain poised and give the supervisor a chance to reply, but do not get into a pointless exchange of drivel and tiresome rhetoric that serves no purpose other than to insult your intelligence. If the supervisor says something completely outrageous, it is best not to respond at all. Stonewall. Be dead silent. No reaction from your lips or on your face.

Be prepared to stand by what you are saying. Recognize that some supervisors may not appreciate it, and you may be terminated. But that hasn't been my experience. You will most likely be the one who will have to end the assignment.

There have been two occasions when I have given similar speeches. Both clients retained my services and things improved to lesser and greater degrees. One place even gave me a birthday cake the following week.

Do not discuss the exchange with other staff members, even if they "overheard," and ask you about it in a sympathetic tone. Don't kid yourself.

Hint: I recommend having this talk just prior to leaving for lunch. When you come back, if you have indeed been doing a good job, you will notice a sense of relief that you came back from lunch and, hopefully, a positive difference in the atmosphere. This gives you and the others in the office a time to settle down before returning to work.

What else can you do? Assuming that you are doing a good job, weigh the pros and cons. If you don't need a steady paycheck and if the assignment is simply too stressful and unpleasant, end it. If the situation is intolerable, call your temporary service, give notice, and ask for another assignment.

If you decide to stick with the assignment, keep on doing a good job. Don't slack off. Just keep cranking out the work. But don't give yourself ulcers or a stroke. No job is worth that.

Do your best, but if quitting time is 5:00, and someone dumps something on you at 4:45 that you cannot possibly finish by 5:00, don't agree to stay over unless you really want to. If you do stay late, make sure you record the time on your time card. Stop cutting your lunch hours short. If you are allowed an hour for lunch, take the full hour and don't feel guilty.

Do your job. Do what you can, as well as you can. And, at the appointed hour, go home (or wherever) and forget about them. Come to work on time, be pleasant, but stop breaking your neck. Why? You will become more frustrated, and maybe even blow your stack one day, and do or say something stupid. Something that you will regret. And that is not good. It really isn't worth it. Do not play their game, remain above it and remain professional. I am not saying that this will always work. What I am telling you is that you will have a much better chance of making it through the game by following my suggestions.

If things don't improve or at least settle down, don't complain or make any more efforts to reach an understanding. You have already tried that. Enough is enough. Get out of there and move on.

It surprises me that many temporaries feel they are powerless. If you are a good temporary, you are anything but powerless. In certain cases, you have more power than the permanent employees. Sure, some people at the job site may see you as powerless. Let them see whatever they want. And you might run into a few people whose attitude says: "Who does she think she is? She's just a temp." Wrong. You are not just a temp—you are a great temp. They are lucky to have you. And most of them know it.

If you weren't doing a good job, they would have gotten rid of you a long time ago. And, as far as other permanent employees are concerned, they will most likely back off if they feel that you might quit. Why? Because they will have to do the work themselves, or they will have to train yet another temporary. And the next temporary might not be a winner. They might get the world's worst temporary (which would serve them right). So, if you are a great temp, don't be conceited about it, but do not ever underestimate yourself.

NOT ENOUGH WORK TO DO

Some people may feel this would be a blessing, but it has its drawbacks. It is not uncommon to have mountains of work to do for several days straight, then experience a slack period where there is nothing to do except wait for a few hours. I have only run into this a couple of times. Always keep busy; read company manuals *not* the newspaper, magazines, or novels; straighten out desks and files; create a manual for the next temporary; explore their computer manual and work at the computer. The fact that there is usually a computer around is a relief for computer junkies. However, lack of work can be unpleasant and boring.

I'm acquainted with one particular temp who possesses

super skills. This woman is a dynamo. Her skills, personality, demeanor, and savvy put her in the class of "Super Temp." She was sent on an assignment which was supposed to involve word processing, typing on a typewriter, setting up files, and answering the telephones. The client told the temporary help company that it was a busy slot, which needed filling for two weeks while the permanent employee was on vacation.

The temporary told me that aside from opening the mail, she was not given one thing to do for the entire two weeks. She was miserable. She said:

I need to feel productive. The days dragged by, and the telephones hardly ever rang. I felt guilty about taking a lunch hour. The bosses didn't seem to mind that I wasn't doing anything. I read every magazine they had. I mentally revised my résumé. I thought of asking for another assignment, but they were very willing to pay a lot of money for a warm body to be there, sit at the desk, open a few pieces of mail, sign for deliveries, and take a few messages. It was somewhat of a respite from the previous (hectic) assignments, but I was bored silly.

It happens.

PERSONALITY CONFLICTS

Sometimes an employer or a permanent employee simply doesn't like the temporary. A confident, self-assured temporary who has been around, does the work, minds her own business, and has no desire to be a permanent employee can really bother some people. Whether they get personally insulted or feel unnecessarily threatened, they will dump work on the temporary, hoping that she will be unable to stand it and will quit. If the temporary doesn't quit and they continue to feel threatened, they may call the service, give some absurd excuse, and the temporary will be informed that her services are no longer required. Period.

OFFICE POLITICS

Read the next sentence three times, and commit it to memory.

DO NOT GET INVOLVED IN "OFFICE POLITICS" AND DISPUTES AMONG PEOPLE AT THE WORK SITE.

Sounds simple, right? Not always. This can be a serious problem because people of all levels will often try to pull you into all sorts of messy situations. Sometimes they will be sly about it, and at other times they will use the subtlety of a sledgehammer.

Keep in mind that you are an outsider—whether you like it or not. If things get ugly, the outsider will be labeled as the troublemaker. It is better just to do your work and keep to yourself. You may be called antisocial, but that's not so bad. If you go to break or lunch with other employees, keep the conversation light—talk about current books or movies.

There is nothing wrong with friendliness, but offices and work sites are often filled with people who have all sorts of hidden agendas. Even seemingly innocent remarks and questions can have unpleasant repercussions. ("Hmm ... how long ago did so and so leave for lunch?, When did you-know-who show up for work this morning? *Do not* buy into these tactics.

Whether you are in a permanent job or on a temporary assignment, you will find that a considerable portion of the workday is spent watching for, wondering about, and talking about such earth-shattering things. And then there are many monologues that sound something like this: "Well, it wasn't my fault. I did my job. So I told her ... then she said ... and I went to Mr. What's-his-face and let him know about it ... blah ... blah ... blah" or variations of the same theme. You get the point.

There are many ways to deal with office politics, scuttlebutt, games—whatever you want to call it. The best way to handle it is to not get involved at all. Sure, you can jump in with both feet and revel in it. If your adrenaline starts pumping when you sense something "going on"— usually something that is none of your business—well, you can skip this section.

But let's assume that you don't like to get involved in or even hear about office politics. What do you do?

First, accept the reality that your job is not to control or change the personalities and character flaws of other people at the work site.

Then, try to ignore it. For example, when Person #1 comes to you and says (or slyly implies) something derogatory about Person #2, you can pretend you didn't hear it. Or look directly at the gossiper and say nothing. Don't smile. Don't frown. Don't shrug. Look at the person and say nothing. This won't win you any friends, but after you do this a few times, Person #1 will get the message and limit conversations to mandatory business.

You can let it get to you, and talk to your service and your supervisor at the job site about it. This is usually a mistake; it rarely accomplishes anything positive, and adds to the tension.

Or you can practice what I like to call Diplomatic Side-stepping. This tactic can even be fun, and it works best for me. Let me explain.

Most offices have cliques. Groups that are regarded as, or consider themselves to be, the "in crowd." Right behind that group is usually a smaller group of Malcontents or Wannabes. The Wannabes are people who would like to be, and strive to be, part of the "in crowd." But members of the "in crowd" avoid these leeches. There is very little crossover.

Frequently the Malcontents cluster together and review what has happened over the course of the workday—who said what, what's going on, etc. On many occasions I have walked into the lunchroom where they are hanging out and one of the Malcontents will say something to me, attempting to draw me into their gossip. I have learned to respond tactfully. Sometimes with noncommittal humor ("Oh, you people are terrible!" followed by a laugh). This keeps me out of the middle, eliminates tension, and protects me from future accusations because I said nothing of substance. In my experience, this has paved a much smoother way than a disdainful, "I beg your pardon, but I prefer not to get involved in your office gossip. I am here to do a job."

This diplomatic sidestepping routine is not 100% effective. In fact, on a few occasions I have been called a smart aleck and a few other things even less endearing. But that is usually because someone finally realizes that I am uninterested in their "crises" and hidden agendas. Being considered a smart aleck is a small price to pay.

Occasionally, people will press until you are forced to be direct, at the risk of offense. I have had to come out and state, "If you are having a problem with John/Jane, that is really between the two of you." This won't win many friends, but these are not people I would choose as friends anyway. You are only there for a short period of time. If possible, avoid becoming involved in these discussions in any way.

Let's face it: office politics is simply a sophisticated version of the games that were played in junior and senior high school. We are older, better educated, and better dressed, but the games continue. Everyone seems to have his own agenda. The wise employee will avoid becoming involved.

Quiz

Remember that sentence I asked you to repeat three times? Did you memorize it? Good for you! (Just checking.)

"FITTING IN"

It is true that temporaries are often excluded, but what do you do when the permanent employees try to include you beyond your comfort level? This is touchy. No one likes to be rejected and some people deeply resent being rejected by a temporary employee. If you do not want to become any closer to a coworker or group of coworkers, you could say something like, "Thanks, it's really nice of you to invite me but I have a lot of things going on right now and cannot join you." This sounds much better than "I'm sorry. I'm a busy person with my own friends and interests."

Once, while I was working at a long-term assignment, one of the secretaries mentioned to me that a previous temporary always expected to join her for lunch. She told me she felt smothered by the other temporary. I assured her that would not be a problem with me as I valued my private time during lunch. When it became clear to her that I was telling the truth and that I really was not interested in having lunch with her, she became slightly insulted.

Of course, it is nice to be treated like a permanent staff member. And yes, occasionally I enjoy having lunch with coworkers. Sometimes I go to lunch or take breaks with other temporaries. Occasionally. But there are limits.

I learned many years ago that it was best not to become too closely involved with work associates, especially on temporary assignments. And, like some of you, I also learned the hard way not to cry on a shoulder that belongs to anyone I work with every day. Innocuous, polite chatter and an occasional lunch are fine. Anything beyond that tends to make me uneasy.

While working at temporary assignments, I have often been asked to participate in various social functions, such as birthday parties, celebratory lunches, drinks after work, dinner, etc. It is nice to be asked, but I usually politely decline. Mostly because I have other things to do. Sometimes because I just don't want to participate. There have been some exceptions, but not many. I prefer to choose my own friends and get acquainted with individuals as opposed to groups.

Often, the people I work with find it hard to accept my

refusal—no matter how nice I am about it. They go on and on about it: "You are welcome. You are one of us. Why not? Don't you like us?" But rarely do I accept. One group of people found it hard to comprehend that my evening college classes (or any other plans I had for the evening) were more important to me than being with them. When I do join someone for lunch, I steer the conversation to safe topics (movies, good books, car repairs, the outrageous price of clothing). When they try to bring me into a discussion about people at the work site, or start nosing around in my personal life, I have all kinds of ways of deflecting it— look at my wristwatch, contact lens attack, gotta run an errand, even pretend to choke on my sandwich.

No matter what plans you may have, or what may be going on in your life, most people at the work site will find it hard or impossible to believe that you have no desire to become a permanent fixture. Even when you tell them that you are satisfied doing temporary work, that you prefer to have some time to yourself at lunch, they don't really hear you. They don't believe you, and are often trying to be nice.

For example, in 1990 I was asked to do some data entry work for a few weeks at the corporate offices of a retailer. The assignment went well, but my supervisor made it a point, several times, to tell me they didn't have any vacant data entry positions. Perhaps he just wanted to make sure that I didn't count on anything. But the fact was that I was not interested in being a permanent data entry operator— there or anywhere else.

There are times when a temporary employee and a client company turn out to be a perfect match. That's great. And some client companies seek temporaries with the understanding that if things work out for all concerned, the temp will be hired as a permanent employee. That is also great. What I object to is the automatic assumption that every temporary employee wants to continue working at that particular company, in that particular position, for life. It just ain't necessarily so.

One exceptionally bright temporary I worked with put it a different way. She happened to be a documentary film maker who was working on her Master's degree. One day during coffee break she came up to me at the vending machines and said: "These people slay me. I have worked here a month and they seem to be sure that I want to spend my life here. The truth is that if I had to work with some of them on a permanent basis, I would gladly murder them."

That is a bit extreme, but I knew exactly what she meant and how she felt.

Among more than sixty temporary assignments I have filled, there were only four instances (as of this writing) where I wanted either that position or another comparable one in that particular organization. But they had hired someone else prior to calling in a temporary, had a hiring freeze, my background and skills didn't match their needs, or the salary wasn't in the ballpark.

NOSINESS

People are often overly solicitous or curious about your personal life. The most common question is: "Why are you doing temporary work?" or, the (supposedly) more innocent: "So ... do you just do temporary work, or what?" I find that a good answer to that is "I do a lot of different things for different reasons." Of course, I smile as I say it, but they usually get the message. Don't feel that you have to explain, justify, and rationalize why you are doing temporary assignment work.

One of the more unpleasant assignments in my memory was for a government organization that hired me and three other temporary word processors for what was supposed to be a three-month assignment. One of the temporaries became close with a clique of permanent employees — the "in crowd." First of all, this woman clearly wanted to be part of the gang. She brought in pictures of her children and hung them in her work area, even though she knew the job was temporary. She volunteered information about her life that most people would be embarrassed to tell anyone — evictions, garnishments, being fired from various jobs, allegations of sexual harassment — the list was endless. The permanent employees pretended to sympathize, but whenever the temp was outside listening range, they rolled their eyes and ridiculed her. Not much work was getting done. What a mess.

This organization had recently come under fire for using so many temporary employees and wasting money in general. There was some real bad publicity about it in the newspaper and on television. But it was also obvious, to me and to other temps, that the permanent employees were slacking off and taking advantage of the situation. One day, we were told that, due to budgetary factors, we would all be terminated at the end of the week. Several hours were spent apologizing and explaining. But while all the hand wringing was taking place, the savvy temps (myself among them) took a break, went to the pay phones, and lined up more work.

As soon as we returned, several people came up to us and asked: "What will you do?" (with the rest of your life) The question was accompanied with furrowed brows and the familiar "you poor thing" look. I loved it when one temp responded: "Oh, I'll sit at home in my ratty bathrobe and fuzzy slippers and eat bonbons."

Regardless of what you say, people are going to make assumptions and draw their own conclusions about why you are working on temporary assignments. There is nothing you can do about that. It is really nobody's business. You don't have to feel obligated to invent any excuse at all. Don't volunteer information about your romances, finances, children, problems with your landlord, or the juicy details about the real reason you no longer have a permanent job. That can backfire and haunt you in ways that you never imagined.

ABUSIVE SITUATIONS

Don't tolerate abusive treatment from an employer or a temporary help service. You may think, "I have no choice. I was a victim of budget cuts and I lost my job. I'm a single parent with $6.14 to my name." I know about money problems. I also know that your self esteem can take a beating when you have no job and you feel that you will just have to put up with bad treatment until things get better. But don't just put up with shabby treatment. Speak up, and move on as quickly as you can.

If you find yourself in a situation that is truly unbearable, and you are ready to walk off an assignment, take a deep breath. Go to a telephone (preferably a pay phone away from others) and call your service. Tell them what the problem is. If you need to get out, say so and give them a definite time so that they can find a replacement. Don't be persuaded to "stick it out" if it is unbearable, and only you can be the judge of that. Some of my earlier examples show the error of this. Of course, it is reasonable for the service to ask you to finish the day in order to allow them time to search for a replacement. If the service is worth its salt, it will release you as soon as possible and give you another assignment. Remember: Call the service first, give reasonable notice, *then* walk. And don't look back.

I know of some instances where temps were miserable on job assignments, and the service asked them to keep a "journal" and document everything. I know of an instance wherein a coordinator told a temp, "We need for you to prepare a report. Document everything: who said what, who did whatever, who was a witness. Dates, times, etc. In case there is a lawsuit, or the client refuses to pay the bill, we will need all the evidence we can get." I don't think a temporary should be responsible for going through all that. If the temporary help company wants documentation, and if they are doing their job, *they* should be doing the documenting. Others may not consider this a problem, and may even find it challenging or exciting. Personally, I feel this is the responsibility of the service, not the temporary.

UNUSUAL PROBLEMS

There are other problems, sometimes unusual ones, that often have nothing to do with workload, per se.

I am now going to give examples of how to handle some of these from my own experience with two very different problem situations at temporary assignments.

The Evacuation

A service called me to see if I was interested in a two- to three-week assignment as a secretary in a large organization. I wasn't pleased with the low pay rate, but I had nothing else lined up. I accepted, even though this particular service had a bad habit of misrepresenting assignments to its temporary workers.

When I arrived at the Human Resources Department of the client firm, I had to wait for over an hour for someone to come and take me to the area where I was to be working. Eventually, I was taken to a large area that was crowded and noisy. People were literally falling over each other. And soon they were tripping over me. My desk was a small, rickety typing stand in the middle of an aisle. I had to hold material that I was typing from in my lap. There was a huge plant sticking in my face. The leaves were actually brushing against my cheeks. There was no way to move to another area. There literally was not one square foot of extra space. I asked if the plant could be moved, and was told that there was no place to move it. (The plant was a permanent fixture —I was not.)

My job was to type thousands of nine digit numbers onto small adhesive labels. The typewriter was not functioning properly. Someone told me that if I hit it a certain way before pressing the return, it would work. I stuck it out for a couple of hours, but the thought of working like this for weeks made me miserable.

After I had been diligently trying to type for two hours, I smelled gas and heard a screeching alarm. An announcement came over the intercom that there was a gas leak and the building would have to be evacuated. I grabbed my coat and belongings, and, along with everyone else, left the building.

For about an hour, everyone waited outside. I walked to a pay phone and called the service. I told them that I was displeased with the assignment and why, and that I wanted to end it. I also told them about the evacuation. My coordinator simply said, "Well, go on to lunch and check in with us this afternoon. We heard that the building may not be safe to enter for a few hours. Call us later and let us know how it is going. Hang in there. Bye!"

Instead of going to lunch, I touched base with another service. They had a good assignment for me, which I accepted. I called and terminated the other assignment. This did not make the first service happy, but it was too much.

In retrospect, I realize that I should have finished out the day so that the employer could have found a replacement. But in that moment, I didn't feel that was possible. Whenever possible, stay for the day but make it clear to your service and to the client company that you will not be returning the next day and why.

Tote that Bale, Lift that Barge, Bring My Lunch

A temporary help service called me to fill a one-week secretarial assignment in a small branch office of an insurance company. The woman who was my supervisor greeted me and showed me the basics of what I was to do. Then she came out to my desk several times an hour and gave me her version of staffing problems and recent office turnover. She seemed to relish these problems and was not a pleasant person to be around. For most of the work day, there were only the two of us in the office.

At this time, I was taking night classes and using my lunch hour to study. My supervisor asked me daily to bring lunch to her when I returned from my lunch. There were plenty of places within walking distance and she could easily have gone out. Of course, she paid for her own food, but I felt this was an imposition on my time, but, mistakenly, I agreed and picked up lunch for her the first two days of my assignment. I called my service and cleared with them that it was not my duty to act as her catering service.

On the third day, I truly did not have time to stop and get her lunch. When I let her know that I was leaving for lunch, my supervisor grabbed her wallet and said: "Bring me a double cheeseburger — no onions, a large order of fries, and a chocolate shake." She then told me to stop at a convenience store on the way back to pick up a couple of candy bars. I ignored the five dollar bill she was trying to thrust at me and said, "I don't have time for that." Hands on hips, she raised her eyebrows and asked: "Why not? I don't see what difference it should make. As long as we are paying you." I didn't respond. I just said that I would be back in an hour and left.

The following day, she again asked me to pick up her lunch. I told her I did not have the time and did not want to. She was even more unpleasant. During my lunch, I called my service, filled them in and confirmed that I would stay the week, but no longer.

On Friday, when she signed my time card, I pointed out that "since this is my last day," I needed to show her a few things about the tasks I had been working on. She gave me an incredulous look and said: "You aren't coming back?" I reiterated that the agreement was for one week, and that week was over. She put her hands on her hips, pursed her lips, and stared at me for a while. When time came for me to leave, she didn't say "Thanks," "Goodbye," "Drop dead," or anything else. Neither did I. I just left, happy that the assignment was over.

It is important to stress that I am not advocating temporaries ever "walk out" on an assignment. I know that is unprofessional. But neither client companies nor temporary help companies should expect a temporary worker to put up with abuse. A temporary worker often has to put up with more unpleasant work than permanent employees, but too frequently the line between inconvenience and abuse is crossed.

Note that whenever I encounter problem situations, I keep the temporary service informed about what is going on. Some services handle "problem" clients, "problem" employees, and "problem" situations better than others. There are temporary help services and assignment coordinators who will move mountains for you, and others will leave you whistling in the wind. Once you have sorted them out, drop the services that do not support their temporaries.

8

Other Opinions

ROUNDTABLE DISCUSSION WITH TEMPORARIES

I conducted a "roundtable" discussion with six other tempo-rary employees. All of them have been working on tempo-rary assignments for at least six months and one has been a temp for seven years. I posed a few general questions about life as a temporary, and their responses follow. (Names have been changed by request.)

Karen: *What do you see as the biggest problems faced by temporary employees?*

Sandy: Most companies are not prepared for a temporary. They expect you to be able to walk in the door and know everything about their operation. When you don't, or if you "mess up," it is never their fault.

(Sandy worked for two years for temporary help compa-nies, then developed her own clientele. She now works strictly freelance.)

Richard: The computer revolution has been a mixed bless-ing. Although I know six different computer software pack-ages, there have been many instances when the service has told me that the client uses one software package, and when I arrive at the job site I find out it is something different.

Brenda: Generally speaking, companies want to get all they can out of you as cheaply as possible. I admit that several unpleasant experiences with client companies and temporary service companies have left me somewhat bitter about doing temporary assignment work. For example, one supervisor wanted me to copy all of the company's computer software on disk for him so he could take it home. He said that he was in the process of starting his own business on the side. I told him that was copyright infringement, and I wanted no part of it. There is a tremendous amount of abuse (by client companies and temporary services), but meanwhile I have to earn a living.

Judy: The temporary who relies solely on one service will have a problem getting good, steady job assignments. I think it is mandatory to register with at least three services. I am registered with five services, and they keep me busy. I really haven't had any bad experiences.

Paula: Without a doubt, the biggest problem for me has been that permanent employees slack off when a temporary is brought in. I had to learn to wear "blinders," ignore what others may or may not be doing, and just do the best I could.

Don: I work at industrial assignments. Most of the permanent employees treat me like their own personal flunky. I have to do the tasks they don't want to do. But I rarely complain about it because, frankly, I don't want any hassles.

Karen: *Let's talk money. Without quoting specific dollar amounts, are you satisfied with your earnings on temporary assignment work?*

Sandy: I am very comfortable.

Richard: Although I would like to make more, I honestly feel that I am fairly compensated.

Brenda: The pay is "OK"; however, I feel that temporary help companies could take a smaller cut and still make a nice profit.

Judy: I feel that I am slightly underpaid.

Paula: Financially, things are often tight. This is partially because I often have days (or weeks) go by when I don't have a job assignment.

Don: I feel that temporaries are underpaid. It is often tough (or impossible) to get a raise.

QUESTIONNAIRE RESPONSES FROM TEMPORARIES

In addition to sitting with the temporaries above, I sent questionnaires to temporaries in different parts of the country.

Here are the questions I asked:

1. How long have you worked as a temporary?
2. How many services are you currently registered with?
3. Are job assignments steady, or do you experience gaps?
4. What type(s) of work do you/have you performed on assignments?
5. Are you currently seeking a permanent job?
6. What are some of the disadvantages of being a temp?

7. What are some of the advantages?
8. Do you feel that client companies treat you fairly?
9. Do you have an interesting story or experience to share?

I instructed participants not to give names of specific temporary help companies or any information that would identify client companies. Here are some of the replies.

Longmont, Colorado

Pam Howell has done temporary work for a year and a half. She is registered with only one service, and she reports that job assignments are steady. She has done various types of work on temp assignments: data entry, shipping/receiving, exposition contract confirmation. Pam feels that client companies treat her fairly.

ADVANTAGES. *Before I worked as a "temp," I would have been VERY uncomfortable going to a restaurant alone. But now I'm comfortable doing that. PLUS ... you meet a lot of nice people "Joe Public" doesn't see.*

DISADVANTAGES. *You never are part of the "gang"—the "group"; you eat a lot of lunches alone.* Pam also points out that the company you are temping for feels bad about not needing your services any longer. She tries to assure them that she has another assignment waiting for her.

Honolulu, Hawaii

Marvalene K. Adams has temped for five months, and she is registered with one service. Job assignments have been steady. She works on assignments as a typist, receptionist, and file clerk, and she is currently seeking a permanent job.

ADVANTAGES. *(1) Being able to go into any office and fit in with very little training. (2) Weekly paychecks are very nice. (3) Your temporary service does all the legwork. You stay home and wait for the call.*

DISADVANTAGES. *Meeting nice people and having to leave after a short period of time.*

Marvalene feels that client companies treat her fairly most of the time. However, she says, *One company I worked for constantly blamed "temps" for their own inefficiency.*

Leslie Fellhoelter is also from Honolulu, and has been working at temporary assignments for approximately six years. She works intermittently; however, assignments are steady, and she is registered with only one service. She works at clerical assignments — typist, receptionist, and accounting clerk, and she vividly recalls the anxiety that she felt when she went on her first assignment.

Broken Arrow, Oklahoma

Nancy Zelnick has worked for one temporary service for about six months. Her first assignment lasted for four months, and the other assignments have been for one to two weeks, with a couple of days in between assignments. She has performed a variety of duties on assignments.

Nancy indicated that although she is not actively seeking a permanent job, she might be interested if the right job came along.

ADVANTAGES. *I enjoy being able to take time off if my son is in a school program or if I have a doctor's appointment. I am enjoying trying different kinds of work, before I decide what I want to do permanently.*

DISADVANTAGES. *No benefits (health insurance, sick leave, vacation, profit sharing, retirement). She also said that the social advantages (friendships, being part of a group working toward a common goal) are missing.*

MEDIA PORTRAYAL OF TEMPORARIES

How does the media portray temporary employees? Let's take a quick look at some of the more current examples.

Jungle Fever

In Spike Lee's 1991 movie *Jungle Fever*, one of the primary characters is a temporary employee. There was one scene which I found particularly disturbing. For those of you who didn't see the movie or perhaps don't remember the scene, I'll outline it for you.

The central character, Flipper, is a married architect who is having an affair with his secretary, a temporary who works for a service. Flipper's brother, Gator, is a drug addict and, quite frankly, a bum. Gator stops by to see his brother and he meets the girlfriend, Angie. She leaves the brothers alone to talk. When Flipper tells Gator that Angie is a temp, Gator sneers and says something to the effect that Flipper should try to do better. This scene reminds the viewer of an earlier one in which Flipper told Angie that he found it strange that she was doing temp work. He said: "I would think you could do so much better."

With all due respect to Spike Lee and the movie, as a temporary I was offended. It bothered me that a character who had no admirable qualities whatsoever, who was a thief and a drug addict, looked down his nose at a temporary employee.

"The Young and the Restless"

Millions of people watch (or tape) soap operas every day. I happen to be a fan of "The Young and the Restless." In April of 1992 I took special notice of a scene that took place in one of the episodes:

Lauren Fenmore is the gorgeous, high-powered President and CEO of a multi-million dollar retail business. Paul Williams is a sexy, nice guy detective, who also happens to be Lauren's ex-husband. Lauren and Paul frequently drop in and visit each other at their offices.

On this particular day, Paul dropped in to see Lauren. He walks into her office and says: "Hi. Marjorie (Lauren's secretary) wasn't at her desk."

Lauren replies: "Marjorie is out with the flu, and the temp they sent is worse than having no one. I sent her on an extended coffee break."

"L.A. Law"

Are you a fan of (or at least familiar with) "L.A. Law"? In the 1991 season premiere episode, the following scene took place:

Arnie Becker arrived at the staff meeting in a snit. His regular secretary, Gwen, was serving on jury duty. A temporary was replacing her. No one had cleared this with Arnie. He was huffing and puffing about being "stuck with a temporary."

In "L.A. Law's" 1991 Christmas episode, one of the plot lines focused on a temporary secretary who "freaked out." At the office Christmas party, she threw her keyboard through the window and threatened suicide.

"Murphy Brown"

Murphy Brown has gone through a parade of temporary secretaries. One of them turned out to be Kramer from "Seinfeld." (Give me strength.)

In the examples above, I am not criticizing the people who are responsible for these shows. What bothers me is that I know they are an accurate reflection of the public's perception of temporary employees and the temporary help industry. I could easily give more examples that indicate the public perception of temporary employees is less than positive.

PUBLIC PERCEPTION OF TEMPORARIES

How does the general public really feel about temporary employees? Let's look at what some "real" people say about temporaries.

I mailed a questionnaire to get feedback about how John and Jane Public feel about temporary employees. Here are the questions I asked:

1. Does your employer use the services of temporary employees?
2. How do you feel when you are told that a temporary is going to be helping out with work overflow or sub-stituting for someone?
3. Regardless of whether or not your employer uses tem-porary employees, what are some of the reasons, in your opinion, that people work at temporary assign-ments?
4. Do you feel that temporaries are treated fairly by peo-ple at the work site? Why or why not?
5. Would you ever consider doing temporary assignment work? (Clerical, general labor, professional, technical, or perhaps as a consultant?)
6. Do you have an interesting story to share? I am espe-cially interested in hearing unusual stories—extraor-dinarily good or bad experiences you have had while working with temps.

Dublin, Ohio

Ray Brown's past employers have used temps from ser-vices. His present employer creates an internal pool of tem-porary workers who are employees.

With regard to how Ray feels when he is told that a tempo-rary is going to be helping out or substituting for someone, he said that he feels: *relieved* that the work will be done, *appre-hensive* about the work being done adequately, and *hopeful* that a good future employee prospect may turn up.

Why do people do temporary work? Here's Ray's opinion: *They do not have full-time, permanent work and they hope to find full-time permanent work. A few [work at temporary as-signments] because they actually only want temporary, part-time work.* Ray feels that, as a general rule, temporaries are treated with courtesy and professionalism.

Ray said he was surprised to learn that temps are some-times paid as little as one-half of what the service actually bills the client. He had some more interesting comments:

Some services use the temporary process as a means of placing employees with a client company permanently for a fee. This is not always disclosed to the temp, and sometimes it is implied when in fact the client company has no intention of hiring any permanent employees. Some client companies use the temp process as a screening device for potential employees. This is rarely disclosed to the temp. In one instance, I observed temps being sent back to the service for unsubstantiated and undocumented reasons, apparently because they had not passed the "screening."

Ray feels that this is abusive and I agree with him.

Columbus, Ohio

David Heilman's employer has had "generally favorable" experiences with temporaries. Heilman says that he would consider doing temporary assignment work if he lost his job and couldn't find permanent work right away.

David shared the following story:

We needed a temporary secretary / receptionist to [fill in] for someone recovering from surgery. The temp was to report to work at 8:00 A.M. on Monday. She called at about 8:30 and said that she was lost, so I gave her specific, detailed directions. She showed up at 11:00 and I asked her about her qualifications. (We needed someone who knew WordPerfect and Lotus 1-2-3.) She didn't, and she threw a fit. I sent her out the door.

I called the personnel office to gripe about the first temporary, and a replacement temp was sent out the next morning. She was bright and had the skills that we needed. She fulfilled her six-week assignment with our office, and was then hired on permanently in another department.

Dublin, Ohio

Linda Brown's employer does not use temporaries from a service. They have a list of substitute secretaries and receptionists, most of whom are found by word of mouth.

In Linda's opinion, the reasons that people work at temporary assignments are:

They only want to work part-time, they are hoping to find full-time employment, they may be new to the city / area, and also schoolteachers have the opportunity to work during summers, spring break, holidays, etc.

She said that she would try to make temporary employees feel comfortable, but would not assign any confidential or in-depth tasks to temporary employees.

Although she has never worked as a temp herself, Linda was a service representative/consultant for two temporary services. At one temporary help company, the job was very frustrating because people would make appointments to come in and test/interview, then not show up or even call to cancel.

Regarding her experience as a representative for the other temporary service, Linda had this experience to share:

The other temporary service was very frustrating. Our boss did not want us to leave the office all day because he feared losing a job order or a client. We ate lunch in the office between phone calls. One time we were brave and we went out to lunch with our supervisor. We got caught! We had turned on the recorder and, lo and behold, who called? The boss! He was quite upset. I felt that the phone was glued to my ear all day. The temporaries who were working on job assignments were calling us on their lunch hours about their paychecks, to complain about the job assignments, or to ask about future job assignments. By the time I got home in the evening, I didn't want to talk to anyone! But we did get an opportunity to get out of the office to deliver Christmas "goodies" to clients and to make service calls—with a cheery "hello, hope all is well" type of attitude. I would not do that type of work again. I love my job now (it is not with a temporary service and I did not find it through a temporary service).

9

To All Employers, Client Companies, and Coworkers

It may sound as though I have been beating up on employers, client companies, and coworkers. I don't mean to. Believe it or not, I sympathize with you. I know how frustrating it can be to train and work with temporary employees. On permanent jobs, as a secretary, as a professional, and also as a supervisor, I had several dreadful experiences with temporaries.

As is customary, the organizations I worked for as a permanent employee never bothered to prepare for a temporary. Even though we all knew that people get sick, go on vacations, and experience emergencies, etc., preparing for a temporary employee was never on the top of anyone's list. We had used a temporary for short-term absenteeism, and management's attitude was: "Just introduce the temporary to everyone, show him/her how to answer the telephones, and we'll take everything else as it comes. No big deal." Indeed, no big deal—as long as nothing goes wrong. And something always goes wrong.

MY OWN WORST EXPERIENCE
WITH A TEMPORARY

Our regular, dependable, efficient secretary experienced a medical emergency one evening on the way home from work. In this particular organization, we had to go through the personnel office to request a temporary. This required forms being filled out and signed, and a staff member from the

—127—

personnel office calling a temporary service. Well, all the bureaucratic nonsense could take a couple of hours or several days. And since we just had the one secretary, the rest of us had to take turns answering phones. Of course, there was a crisis situation—we were all trying to prepare for an executive board meeting. Telephones were ringing, work was piling up, and tempers were short.

At about 1:00 P.M. our temporary arrived. I was given the responsibility of showing her around and training her. From the beginning, there were problems. She walked in with a plastic bag and explained that her lunch had exploded in her car, and she needed a few minutes to clean up the mess and make it edible, because she hadn't eaten lunch yet. (Neither had I.) She didn't know how to use the computer. We had a unique system, and finally determined that it would be best for her to stick to the typewriter. Her typing skills were absolutely horrible, and she was terrible on the telephones. I also think she felt overwhelmed by the large quantity of work that needed to be done.

She kept having to type the simplest documents over and over. She lost several important calls. She had no concept of how to take a message, even though we emphasized that she had to get a name (ask the correct spelling) and a telephone number. She continued just to say: "You had a call a few minutes ago. I don't know who it was. They will probably call back." The boss had instructed her not to bother the computer, since she was not able to use it. But no, she played around with it until (you guessed it) vital documents were wiped out completely. I wanted to curl up into the fetal position and weep.

In addition, our darling temporary was quick to pick up on some of the tension in the office. (It was hard to miss.) She sensed some bad blood between two coworkers. One was male, the other was female. The temp developed a crush on the guy. The temp parked in his office and fed him all kinds of garbage about what his coworker had supposedly said about him. She even told him that she had seen his coworker go through his desk when he was out to lunch. I happened to know this was not true because I usually stayed in the office during lunches and no one went near this guy's desk.

Of course, he got very upset, picked up the ball and ran with it to the boss. This resulted in an amateur three-day "investigation" (which was both comical and infuriating), complete with slamming doors, secret meetings, clandestine telephone calls, and a tremendous screaming match. What a side show.

The thought of putting up with this person posing as a temporary worker for six hours (much less six weeks) made me ill. But I had my own problems and deadlines.

I was waiting for a document to get typed, and she was making no progress whatsoever. I went out to see if I could start proofreading some pages, and she was reading a romance novel. (I should have known we were in for trouble when I saw books on her desk with titles that contained phrases such as "blind passion" and "savage fury.") I went into the boss's office and asked what was going on.

He said: "Well, she told me she has a headache from all the commotion and tension, so I told her she could take it easy."

I was so stunned I couldn't even reply, not that it would have done any good. I was so mad that I was almost tempted to ask her if I could borrow one of her novels. But I did not have that luxury. Later, I noticed that she was writing different combinations of lottery numbers on a steno pad. (Silly me. I thought she might be practicing shorthand.) When I told the boss about this, he told me, in so many words, to butt out. The boss was actually content to let her wistfully read romance novels and pick lottery numbers!!!

Fortunately, a week later, she called her service and asked for another assignment. I could hear her on the phone telling her service all kinds of wild things. Some of those things were true—it was a wild office. But she had contributed to and taken advantage of the craziness. She dumped us. Good riddance. We were able to get a good replacement.

After that experience, and some others that weren't quite as bad, but still frustrating to one degree or another, I compiled a folder of instructions for temporaries. Basic things like names (first and last), titles, how to do the mail, important phone numbers in the department. It really wasn't difficult to put together. The bosses actually thanked me.

ARE YOU CREATING "TEMPORARY CHAOS"?

I am still convinced that much of the chaos, confusion, and negativity associated with the use of temporary workers is generated by the clients themselves. Client companies are usually not prepared for a temporary. It is as if they never heard the phrase "expect the unexpected."

Often, they just call a temporary help company and place a job order. Once they have a temporary, they don't really know what to do with the worker. Sometimes a client will tolerate incompetence because they are so glad to have a warm body, *any* warm body, at the desk. Incredible as it may sound, the philosophy is often that somebody is better than nobody. And nobody wants to be the heavy. They won't ask the temporary service for a replacement because it is frustrating and time consuming to have to train another person. In the example I gave above, the bosses should have given the temporary employee the boot and reported her to the temporary help service, but it was more convenient to leave things as they were.

Does this mean that most companies that employ temporary workers are incompetent jerks and heartless demons? No. In fact, in my experience, there are very few I would label that way. Companies are simply doing things the way they know how to do them. And as I say over and over, throughout this book: they don't usually plan on needing the services of temporary employees.

Most frustrations and fiascoes involve confusion about names, who in the company does what, work that needs to be explained and redone, or instructions on how to use the phones and other equipment, and sort the mail.

And whose responsibility is it to see that the temp is provided with and understands all this information? Yours, the client company.

Now, before you throw this book against the wall or compose a nasty rebuttal, please read on. Remember I want to turn your temporary tribulations into triumphs. Let's get started.

DO YOU REALLY NEED A TEMPORARY?

You might think this is where I am going to tell you to look in the Yellow Pages and what to say when you want to call in a temporary employee. Wrong.

First and foremost, assess the actual need for a temporary worker. Can the excess work be distributed to other employees until things get caught up? Maybe priorities can be rearranged. If you can get along without a temporary, then *don't* place a job order for one.

Temporary help companies would probably like to wring my neck for saying that. While I fight them off with a whip and a chair, allow me to ask you something. As an employer, do you really just want to stick a body with a pulse into a chair and pay money for nothing? I wouldn't think so.

There are some jobs that simply are best not performed by

a temporary. In some situations it would make more sense to transfer a permanent employee into the slot and, if necessary, call in a temp to help out with routine work overflow in another area.

CAN YOU AFFORD A TEMPORARY?

If so, are you willing to pay a fair market rate for services rendered?

This is often where many employers make their first mistake. They call a temporary help company and ask: "What is the lowest rate for a secretary?" or something along those lines. That's not the way to go about it.

If your budget is so tight that you can't (or won't) pay for quality temporary employees either through a service or on a direct freelance basis, then you have no business putting in a job order in the first place. What often happens is that the employer (client company) resents having to pay for an employee on vacation or sick leave, *and* for outside help to fill the vacant position. So the temp often has to bear the brunt in one form or another: either by working for peanuts, or listening to budget woes.

Budget problems can be frustrating, but it simply isn't appropriate — or professional — to complain to a temporary employee about them. If your company resents having to pay for outside help, reallocate the work within, but don't "nickel and dime" your temporary service to death. Once you have come to an agreement to pay a certain rate for the specified services, that's it. Please don't try to renegotiate, especially after the temporary has started work.

HOW DO YOU SELECT A TEMPORARY HELP COMPANY?

If you don't use temporary services on a regular basis, or if it has been a long time since you placed a job order for temporary help, I would strongly advise shopping around. I recommend that all temporary employees do some comparison shopping, and you, the client company, should do the same thing. Call two or three services. Don't automatically go with the most popular service(s) or the first three that you see in the Yellow Pages. It may take a little time, but it is worth it. Ask questions, lots of questions.

Actually, the best time to shop for temporary employees is when you don't need them. If temporary help services are not making regular sales calls on you, contact them. Look in the Yellow Pages under "Employment Contractors—Temporary Help." If you already use temporary services, maybe you have always dealt with one or two services. Perhaps you decide to try a new temporary service. Call a few services, and ask them to send a representative to your office to tell you about their services, policies, and rates.

You say you don't have time? Make the time. The time spent in advance checking out services will save you time and hassle down the road when you need temporary help. If the service balks and says they don't make house calls, thank them for their time and tell them that you will not be using their services. Any temporary help company that does not jump at the chance to get a new client deserves to dry up.

Another method is to visit the offices of a couple of temporary help companies. Unannounced. No, I am not suggesting a surprise attack strategy. But there is certainly nothing wrong with walking in, introducing yourself, and asking to speak with the acting manager about their services. This may be an unorthodox approach, but you will learn a lot about the service by observing the way they operate.

NATS provides the following suggestions to evaluate the services offered by temporary help firms:

- When you buy temporary help services, keep in mind that you're paying for temporary workers backed by a management team. Check the qualifications of the firm's management and service staff through a "customer reference" given by the temporary service.
- Learn how the firm recruits and retains a qualified and reliable work force that's available when you need them. Ask to see their recruitment ads or check the classified section of your newspaper and note what various firms offer potential employees in order to attract top notch temporary workers.
- Are potential employees thoroughly screened, tested, interviewed, and oriented to the temporary help business before being hired?
- Does the firm determine your company's precise temporary help needs and then carefully match that information with fully developed employee work profiles? If so, you'll get the right person or persons for the job. If not, you may pay for a temporary secretary when the job requires a less costly receptionist. Or time may be lost because a receptionist is assigned to your company when first-rate secretarial skills are needed.

- Is the temporary help service a member of NATS? NATS members pledge to abide by all Codes of Good Practices adopted by the association.
- If the firm's staff functions mainly as dispatchers without serious regard for your company's unique requirements, you know you're viewed as just another slot to fill. You might then be assigned mediocre help which requires the constant attention of your expensive supervisory personnel.
- Do the firm's employees usually complete their assignments? Or is turnover frequent, increasing your costs? Here's where a firm's willingness to provide you with customer referrals can be particularly useful.
- Can you rely on the company to fill your last-minute emergencies? How about after-hour emergencies? Can you reach the company after regular business hours? Find out.
- When placing a job order will you get prompt confirmation regarding availability of temporary help or a series of half promises?
- If you're not certain how much temporary help is required for a particular job, what action will the firm take to ensure that you don't underbuy or overbuy? Will their management staff spend time with you and provide correct information so you can accurately define your service needs based on the performance records of first rate temporary help?
- What about insurance? Does the firm carry worker's compensation? What are the policy limits?

HOW DO YOU GET THE RIGHT TEMPORARY?

OK, now you've determined that you need a temporary. You are willing to pay for quality help and you've screened several services, now what?

Let's assume that you have actually spoken with several services. You asked a lot of questions, and received satisfactory answers. You have brochures, cards, and rates. You have established good rapport with a temporary help service, and you feel comfortable calling them and placing a job order.

Throughout this book, I encourage comparative shopping for temporary employees and client companies. I would like to say a few words about what it means to actually place a job order versus "shopping around and obtaining information." When you call a service and place a job order, the coordinator proceeds to match you with an employee who meets your needs and vice versa. The worker is contacted and an agreement is made. What you may not consider is that while you are continuing to "shop around," the temporary employee may have canceled another offer, rearranged plans, and done some personal budgeting. Then, several hours or days later, you call the first service and cancel the order. Or maybe you don't even bother to confirm or cancel the order. So the temporary help company calls you. You say "we changed our mind," or maybe you even volunteer that you decided to go with another service that is giving you a lower rate (but not necessarily better service).

That is shoddy business. As you read this you may be thinking, "So what? The temporary will find something else." Maybe, and maybe not. Meanwhile, you have created problems for a lot of people, and you have left the temporary employee in the lurch.

Would you order wedding cakes from three different bakeries, or cars from two different dealers? Would you "hire" (extend an offer to) four applicants for one job opening, then tell the other three "we changed our mind"?

Temporary help services should crack down on this nonsense. But few that I have talked to are willing to object to it openly. Absolutely no one was willing to go on record and be quoted about it. The temporary help companies are afraid of losing some business. But it still stinks.

What can be done about it? One solution would be to fax an agreement for the client to sign when a job order is actually placed, and require a minimum charge if the order is canceled on a whim or for some frivolous reason. While you, the client, are certainly entitled to change your mind, you should make it clear when placing the initial call that you are not actually placing an order. You should simply say: "We might want a temporary and I would like to obtain some information about your services and your fees. If we want to actually place a job order, we will let you know."

But what do you do when you are ready to place a job order? You need help — extra help, interim help, a replacement, whatever. Other avenues have been explored. The decision has been made to call a temporary service.

Some companies have a system wherein all requests for temporary workers must go through the personnel department or someone else designated to coordinate this function. One of my responsibilities at a former permanent job was to determine the need for and take care of the procurement of temporary workers. This was a very large organization that used lots of temporary employees on a regular basis. Things were getting out of hand; people were indiscriminately picking up the telephone, calling temporary help companies, and placing job orders. Of course, the services loved it, but the allocation for contract services was soon sapped dry.

At my suggestion, and with the support of my supervisors, the organization solved the problem by implementing a policy specifying that "anyone who obtained temporary services without approval would be personally liable to pay for those services." That took care of it.

When you need a temporary, make sure that you are on the same wave length with the office manager, human resources office, purchasing department, or whoever is responsible for actually calling the temporary help service and placing the job order.

It is not good enough simply to say "Get a temporary— now! Just get someone in here who can type and answer phones." A breakdown in communication can be disastrous.

For example, you might specify that you need someone for two weeks who is proficient with WordStar. But personnel tells the temporary service that they need someone for a few days who can perform word processing duties. So someone shows up who only has only worked with the Wang System and WordPerfect. Meanwhile, several hours have been spent training and showing the person various procedures which have nothing whatsoever to do with word processing and, most importantly, the typing (on WordStar), which should have been finished by now, simply is not getting done. So you figure the temp can just use a typewriter. The only problem is that the temp has never seen a Xerox® 6010 MemoryWriter, and it just ran out of ribbon. Is this the temporary worker's fault?

In case you think I am giving you examples from an overactive imagination, I will tell you that I actually witnessed this situation happening. The unfortunate temporary left the assignment — by mutual consent. Later, a replacement was sent. The client had called a different service, but this time they had given the right "specs." Even so, because of what had happened, the work had really piled up, and the temporary was given a brief orientation. The person she was replacing departed early to start her vacation, and the temp was left to fend for herself. She did a wonderful job.

When you place the job order, have some idea as to how long you will need the services of a temporary, and try to be as specific as possible—one day, two weeks, six months, etc. The more you specify your needs, the easier it will be for the temporary help service to find someone to suit you.

MAKE SURE THAT YOU ARE READY FOR A TEMPORARY

This is the tough part. You can skim over the first pages of this chapter (go back and read those pages later — you missed some important stuff). But this is the nitty gritty.

I will try to make it as painless as possible. I know, those of you who run companies, manage staffs, supervise departments, and accomplish many great things over the course of the workday may be thinking, "I have a job to do. I have a corporation to run. I cannot be bothered with the petty, trivial details and problems associated with incompetent temporary workers." Maybe you can't, but, by golly, you better see that someone prepares for the unexpected and even the expected, such as vacations and maternity leaves.

Most offices have no clue what is needed to ensure that working with temporaries will be cost effective and efficient.

If you have gotten this far into the book, you must feel that there is some merit in what I have been saying. Please, —stop right now and make a note to yourself: Have explicit, step-by-step instructions typed up *tomorrow*. The instructions should be in clear, readable typestyle.

Maps

If you have a floor plan, provide it to the temporary. This doesn't mean a huge blueprint. If possible, have someone draw a diagram indicating the location of the mail room, copy room, supply area, fax machine, rest rooms, lunchroom, important offices, human resources department, etc. Be sure to include any area that the temporary needs to know about. It doesn't have to be anything fancy — a rough diagram is definitely better than nothing at all.

Who sits where? A temporary does not need or want a detailed plan of the entire building, just the areas he or she will have to negotiate. Far too many companies don't even use nameplates on offices or desks. That's fine — they all know each other. But it is exasperating and inefficient for a temporary to have to run from desk to desk, interrupt people, and ask where a particular person sits or which door leads to the mail room.

Once I was left completely on my own in a huge corporation. This place was truly a maze of identical desks, cubicles, offices, and hallways. I had to stop several people in the corridors and ask if I was within a five-mile radius of the fax machine and Mr. X's office. I cursed my beautiful new high-heeled pumps. And of course, I was given conflicting directions. Somebody always knows a faster route to take — a shortcut. Uh-huh. This was an unnecessary waste of time.

The irony is that some of the most beautifully designed, aesthetically pleasing, state-of-the-art buildings are the absolute worst when it comes to finding your way around. Try to remember what it was like on your first day, roaming around in a labyrinth.

An Alphabetical List of Names

What do most (over 90%) employers fail to provide to temporary employees? A written list of names (first and last), title, department, and telephone extension numbers. The temp should also have a brief description of lines of authority and responsibility, any important information, unusual procedures, idiosyncrasies, and preferences. That alphabetical (by last name) list must be readable.

This list should be alphabetized by *last name* and should include first and last name, title, department, and phone extension numbers.

It shouldn't be small type like this:

Smith, John Research Ext. 4321

This is much better:

Smith, John Research Ext. 4321

Listings should be at least 10 point type (preferably 12 point).

One of the most frustrating and difficult things on the first few days of a new job assignment is learning names. This can be a serious problem if the temp has to handle telephones. What usually happens is that someone will breeze by the front desk and say: "If anyone is looking for me, I will be in the conference room on the third floor." I ask: "And your name is ...?" Then they will say "John" or "Sue," as the elevator door closes. But there are three Johns and two Sues in the office. Someone stops by the desk and says: "Have you seen John in the last few minutes?" Then a caller asks to speak to George (no last name). When I ask the last name, they don't always seem happy about having to tell me. The caller usually could not care less that I have to find George's extension from a list or directory that is alphabetized by last name. Those three (faded) initials on each button of the phone set don't help much if you don't know what they stand for (JJR, LES, FDW, JTW, and so on). And I could personally strangle those smug people who smirk and say "Gee, all you have to do is press a button." Indeed.

I cannot overemphasize the importance of providing a temporary with an alphabetical list of names, last name first. One company provided me with a list of names, alphabetical by *first* name. While this is better than nothing, it is not in itself sufficient. What if a caller asks for Mr. Porter? Such a list should have been accompanied by (or cross referenced with) an alphabetical listing by last name.

Telephones

Type clear, simplified instructions on how to answer and transfer telephone calls. Forget about giving the temporary the 87-page instruction manual that came with the telephones. Remember that there are many different types of phone systems. Just because a temp worked for a couple of days on XYZ phone system eight months ago, there may be a difference between that system and the one in your offices.

Telephones are not as simple as they used to be. They are now sophisticated, and someone should spend some time with the temporary, if possible, actually demonstrating the operation of the telephone system. It's best to practice and do a few dry runs, especially when it comes to transferring calls. Then let the temporary watch you handle a few "real" calls.

The communications industry, especially with regard to the sale of telephone systems and equipment, must be doing very well. Over the course of more than three years of working at temporary assignments, I have never (that's right, never) encountered two identical telephone systems. For the most part, one system has no resemblance whatsoever to any other. What amazes me further is that clients will say: "Are you familiar with the Starbuck XSE6000 system?" in a tone of voice that implies that operation of that system should be common knowledge. Right. When temporaries confess that they have never seen, heard of, or operated the Super Horizon 163 (or whatever), the client often looks at them as if to say, "Oh ... another Neanderthal. I wonder if she has electricity and running water." (By the way, who thinks up the names for some of these systems — rejects from a Star Trek reunion?)

I love technology, but I can't count the number of times

that someone rattled off instructions, turned me loose, then when calls got disconnected or transferred to the wrong person, I could hear someone say "Sorry—we have a temp, and you know how that can be ..."

This isn't the way to run a business. Have some consideration for the temporary worker; i.e., just because your secretary thinks that a particular task is easy does not mean that it will be as easy for someone who has just walked in the door.

A phone listing or directory that is out of date is worthless. Ideally, the phone list should be cross referenced with a list of departmental extensions, in alphabetical order by department (Accounting, Human Resources, Maintenance, Research, Security, etc.). It would be helpful to know that "Jo" is a female and "Terry" is a male. ("She isn't in her office. Oops, sorry ... I mean he ...")

In an area where more than one person answers telephones, it is important to define the ring protocol. Does the temporary pick up on the first, second, or third ring? Do certain lines automatically roll over to another area? When do the phones roll over and where do they bounce to? Is the temporary supposed to buzz people on the intercom, hold all calls, or walk into offices with a note saying that so and so is holding? What about calls from the top echelon; do staff members take those calls no matter what? And if staff members cannot be found, do they prefer to be "in a meeting," "on another line," "not at their desk," "out to lunch," or "not available"? I found out the hard way that this can be a very touchy issue. I have seen people get chewed out simply because they told someone that a staff member was out to lunch.

Sometimes the most efficient, best organized secretaries, office managers, etc., leave notes about clients, special projects, "tips on what to do if," the fact that I should interrupt John (regardless of what he is doing) if a call comes in from (whoever), letting me know that I can call Lisa at Ext. 347 if I have a problem, etc. Knowing this kind of information is really helpful.

If your organization is large, you probably have a directory (is it current?), and some type of annual report or other document that lists names, titles, addresses, telephone numbers, and fax numbers of other offices. Make sure that it is nearby. The temporary will probably need it.

Mail

Is mail supposed to be opened and stamped in? Should the

date stamp go on the front of a piece of mail or on the back? Should envelopes be discarded or attached to the piece of mail? Or does it matter, as long as the date stamp does not obliterate other information? Should mail be logged in?

How is mail to be delivered/routed? What about pieces of mail that are addressed to former employees or to "President," "CEO," "General Manager"?

Recently I made a "command performance" (went on a job assignment where I had worked before, and the client company remembered me and asked for me by name when they placed the job order). I had really enjoyed working at this particular company. For my return assignment with them, I was told to report to one of their branch offices at a different location. Several people I had met before were there, and that was nice. I was filling in for a secretary who was taking a day off.

At the previous assignment with this company, I remember being pleased that they were reasonably well prepared for a temporary employee. They had asked me to come in for a half day and work with the secretary I was replacing. They had prepared an alphabetical employee listing with phone extension numbers, and also a departmental listing showing who works in which department.

However, at the branch office, they weren't nearly as prepared for me. Perhaps they felt that since I would only be there for one day it wasn't necessary. And they did ask me to come in for a couple of hours to work with the secretary I was filling in for.

The telephone system at this office was strange. But the secretary (a very patient woman) warned me about it, and we practiced for a while. There was no intercom system — this necessitated getting up and finding people. And the secretary said she would try to draw me a diagram/map of who sat where (she volunteered — I didn't ask for it). Unfortunately, she did not have time to do that. It really would have helped. I got lost a few times the next day on my way to the copy room, rest room, and mailboxes. And this branch office was much larger than their office in which I had worked previously.

There was an alphabetical listing of employees, but no indication of which department people worked in. This became a real frustration when I worked on a relatively large mailing. I had to interrupt my supervisor several times and ask questions. (She was very understanding.) Then I went to the mailboxes. The mail slots were labeled with names of

To All Employers, Client Companies, and Coworkers **141**

departments — Accounting, Administration, Customer Service, etc. — instead of names of people. This made the task more difficult and time consuming that it should have been. Of course, a temp knows that sometimes you have to use common sense. For example, I knew that mail for the president of the company went into the box marked "Executive Office," but it was still frustrating.

Postage Meters and Machines

If the temporary is going to be responsible for using the postage meter, make sure that simple instructions, step by step, are written up. Postage machines and meters can be tricky. It is no fun to wrestle with one at 4:50 P.M. when you're trying to get things ready for the 5:00 pickup. Of course, it's also good to go through the process with the temp, but if something goes wrong, it will rarely happen during the training period. Some offices have a small card with instructions placed near the postage meter.

Stationery

The temporary should have a sample of the different types of stationery, letterhead, memo paper, envelopes, and mailing labels. She should be given instructions as to what type of document goes on what type of paper. Show the temp where additional supplies of stationery are kept. Don't just say "back in the supply room." That can mean a shelf in a small closet next to the desk or a warehouse back in never-never land.

If the temp is going to be setting up correspondence, she should be told if you have an established format. Format includes: number of line spaces between the header and the date, whether or not to indent the paragraphs, or justify the right margins, etc. This part is easy. Simply provide copies of actual letters and memos. Kudos to those places that keep notebooks with samples of various types of letterhead, signature blocks, and memos. These are great because they show the preferred format and signature blocks. Personal preferences often vary within the same company. Some people want "Ph. D." or "PH.D." or "Esquire" or "Esq.," and some don't. Some people want their title under their name, others prefer to add the name of the company and department, and there is always the dilemma of "Very truly yours" versus "Sincerely."

Supervision for the Temporary

Make sure that other staff members have no doubt about

who is supervising the temporary worker. Only that supervisor should be authorized to assign work to the temp. All assignments should be channeled through that person. No work should be slipped to the temp on the sly. Not even a "short" letter—forget it.

Other employees should be aware that just because a temporary is being brought in, this is not a signal for them to slack off or dump their work on the temporary. This is not the time for everyone to blow the dust off the work they don't want to do.

Permanent employees frequently take it upon themselves to make sure that the temporary worker has plenty of work to do. This can really be a problem, because the temporary worker is put into the position of taking instructions/orders from several different people. There is always the potential for mixed messages if several different people are giving tasks to temporaries and pulling them in several different directions. When this happens, some things are just not going to get done, or tasks will not get done correctly. Of course, the temporary employee and the temporary help service will be blamed for any and all mistakes.

Instruct temporaries that if other employees attempt to give them work, the supervisor should be notified immediately. This has happened to me far too many times. I can be in the middle of a project, and someone will come and give me something to type (always a "short" emergency letter that has to get in the mail today) or ask me to make thirty double-sided copies of a 100-page manual "when I get a chance." Most of the time their definition of short differs substantially from mine. To me, a "short" letter is one typed page or less. But more importantly, what they never consider is that if several people have asked me to bang out several short letters, it will be impossible to finish the project that I started on before all the interruptions.

The supervisor should nip this in the bud. If the temp is being stretched too far while trying to learn everything and please everyone at once, nothing is going to get done right.

The designated supervisor should be the one who signs the time card. If the temporary has mistakenly charged you for time not worked, point it out and make a correction. Mistakes can be made. I made a simple error in addition once, and the supervisor corrected it. I felt embarrassed, but I simply apologized and it was no big deal. This is very different from the "Time Card Torture" game I spoke of earlier.

Filing

Things can and will get lost—even by the most efficient, reliable permanent employees. After the temporary is gone (or even while he is there), who do you think will be blamed for filing foul-ups—the permanent employee or the temporary? I think you know the answer to that.

It is better to have a temporary pull files and then put them in a stack for someone else to replace, even if you have a simple filing system. I don't need to tell you what problems ensue when files are lost or misfiled. On the other hand, putting invoices, correspondence, reports, etc., in chronological order within a folder or notebook is a more appropriate task for a temporary.

I always try to leave a manila folder with copies of correspondence that I have typed for the regular permanent person to review upon his return. I always save fax cover sheets and fax transmittal confirmations. When necessary, I attach a note: "John, Sue Burns asked me to give this to you." "Sent copies of this to all department heads." It will be appreciated. Who needs to come back from vacation and try to figure out where this came from and what was done with that letter, and whether or not the monthly report was faxed?

Computer Equipment

Even if the temporary is proficient with the type of hardware and software used, it is not wise to require the temporary to perform fancy footwork and sophisticated manipulations on the first day. Even if you get a computer junkie who loves to try new things on the computer, instruct the person to stick to the basics. Computer hardware and software have a multitude of variations. Even keyboards differ. And it is no fun to find out that somebody has customized something. It can take several people endless hours to figure out variations that someone (who at the moment is in the hospital giving birth or sunning on the beach in Maui) has plugged into the system. That is, *if* they can figure it out—sometimes it just cannot be done.

The temporary should be told how to turn on/off the equipment (computers and peripheral equipment such as printers), and in which directories and sub-directories new documents should be created. Remember that sooner or later someone is going to have to retrieve those documents. Some companies use a document code and/or numbering system that is actually printed on the document itself at the bottom. Most businesses take it for granted that just because a document is "in the computer" it can be found quickly. They find out later, the hard way, that nothing could be further from the truth.

One law firm that I work for asked me to put all the documents I created onto a floppy disk. This was smart. I was instructed to assign document names according to the last name of the client and the day's date. (For example, a letter to Ms. Barbara Jenkins was called JENKINS.3-2 or JENK1129. When my assignment ended, the regular secretary was able to look over the documents quickly, copy them onto the hard disk, and rename and arrange them in her own directories and sub-directories. This did not require any more of my time and saved the permanent employee from having to guess where to find these files. I cannot overemphasize the importance of leaving a clear trail for the returning employee.

Deliveries

What are the procedures for package deliveries? Should the temp notify the addressee, the addressee's secretary, or just put them in the mailboxes? Are packages to be checked in? Is it ever necessary to open a delivery?

Special Procedures

Are there any special procedures to be followed at the beginning and end of the day? Turn on/off equipment, lights, check the fax machine, replenish supplies, lock filing cabinets, etc. Are there security measures to be followed? Remember, you and your employees are familiar with special procedures and may forget to go over those things that seem second nature to you now.

Orientation

Many companies assign someone to work with the temporary employee for awhile, and this person (regardless of how nice she may be) usually fails to realize that no one can absorb everything all at once, or even in one day. Sometimes I have taken notes (I always bring my own note pad and pens). Often the person who is orienting me will hand me a small pad and expect me to jot down all kinds of instructions while they talk a mile a minute. Of course, they are also thinking about all the things on their own desks that aren't getting done. They forget that it took them months, sometimes years, to learn what they are expecting me to absorb in an hour.

If at all possible, have the temporary work with the person he/she will be replacing for a day (such as the Friday before the permanent employee starts vacation). This in itself will minimize confusion. Otherwise, the temporary is going to have to interrupt other staff for questions, directions, etc. And I know all too well, that although people say it is OK to ask questions, they often complain to other employees: "I'm behind in my own work. On top of everything else, now I am the lucky one who has to deal with a temp—Yuk!"

It is important to introduce the temporary employee to people she will be working for and interacting with on a regular basis. This may *not* always be possible if staff members are tied up in meetings, traveling, or otherwise unavailable. However, it is not necessary to waste valuable learning/orientation time introducing the temp to everyone who happens to pass by, especially if the assignment is short term. People tend to introduce themselves at the coffee machine or in the course of normal interaction during the work day. The temp is not going to be able to remember everyone's name on the first day, and it just adds to the confusion. This can really be mind boggling in larger companies. The person who is making the introductions may think it simple common courtesy to introduce the temp to everyone. Although "unnecessary" introductions are not a terribly common problem, it does happen often enough to warrant mentioning.

Break Policy

If the temp is in a position where telephone coverage is needed during lunch and trips to the rest room, make sure that a relief person is provided. It is not fair to make the temporary go around and ask people for permission to go to the rest room. A mutually acceptable lunch and break schedule should be agreed upon at the beginning of the assignment.

On several assignments, I have been at the front desk position where I have had to have someone relieve me. Several people assured me "If you need to go to the ladies' room, just call me. I'll be glad to answer the phones." But when nature called, those people were too busy or simply nowhere to be found.

Written Instructions

It is not necessary to write a book or to insult someone's intelligence. But the importance of written instructions for temporaries cannot be overemphasized. For those of you who have already done this: I commend you, and I thank you on behalf of all temporaries.

Right now I am looking at my log of job assignments, from 1985 through 1992. Of all the temporary assignments I have worked at (either through a temporary help service or on a freelance basis), only three companies were actually prepared for a temporary. (These companies and the people who prepared the instructions for temporaries deserve a trophy.) A few other companies (six) were reasonably well prepared. The others didn't even come close. A whopping 94% of the client companies were not prepared to some greater or lesser extent. Only *three* companies, that is about 6%, were prepared.

Either: (1) they gave no instructions and temporaries were left to fend for themselves; (2) they gave information that was essentially useless; (3) they didn't give enough information; or (4) they gave conflicting information by way of several different people. In my experience, number 4 is the worst. Mixed messages = mass mayhem. That is not good. In fact, it is pathetic and inexcusable.

So you agree with me so far. And you or someone else in your office is going to prepare an Instruction Guide for Temporaries. Where do you begin?

Here is a review of the process from placing the order to a sample of the written instructions.

Let's create a company called Karen's Company, Inc. The President and CEO is Karen Mendenhall (of course!). My company (I like the sound of that) provides word processing and other computer services for individuals and small businesses. I employ sixteen people.

When the job order is called in to a temporary service, they will be given the following information:

The receptionist is going to go on vacation for two weeks, and we will need a receptionist with word processing skills. The software package is WordPerfect 5.1. We would like someone with a minimum speed of 60 words per minute; however, we are more interested in someone who can think and handle interaction with the public. The only projects to be given to the receptionist for typing are rough drafts (from hand-written copy) and other material for in-house use only.

The main duties will consist of telephone answering (which can get hectic at times), mail sorting, and greeting clients and visitors. We want someone who has a professional appearance and demeanor, and a pleasant telephone voice.

We are located at 234 West Main Street on the corner of Main and Fairgate. It is the one-story brick building next to The Ming Dynasty Restaurant, and free parking is in the rear of the building. We are also on the bus line. The hours are 8:30 to 5:30 with one hour for lunch and two fifteen minute breaks. We have a lunchroom with a refrigerator, a microwave, and vending machines. There are several restaurants and fast food chains nearby. The temporary will report to and be supervised by Barbara Ives, who will sign the time cards. We want the person to come in on Friday to work for a full day with our permanent receptionist, Connie Larrimer.

At this point the temporary help company is asked to repeat the job specs, so that we are sure we understand each other.

When the temporary employee arrives, Connie will introduce herself and notify Barbara. Barbara will show the temporary around the office. She will show her the location of the coat closet, rest room, copy machine, fax, coffee machine, vending machines, and lunchroom. The temporary will be introduced to all staff. This is a small company and the temporary receptionist will interact with every employee.

The temporary will then work with Connie at the front desk. The temp is given our company brochure and Connie tells her a few things about the company. She will provide printed "Instructions for Temporaries" which includes an alphabetical staff listing and other miscellaneous instructions. Barbara has made it clear that she will deliver and collect any typing assignments. The temp will not be given typing assignments by anyone else. If this happens (and it better not), the temp should notify Barbara or Karen Mendenhall immediately.

Connie will instruct the temporary on how to answer and transfer calls, and how to handle various situations that come up during the course of the day. The temporary will be encouraged to take notes and to ask as many questions as necessary.

The Instructions for Temporaries are updated whenever there is a staff or procedural change. The document is stored in the computer, and the Administrative Assistant and Secretary also keep copies of the document. They composed a similar document for their own jobs, just in case it is needed. Everyone in the office knows where the Instructions for Temporaries documents are filed.

Here is a sample of the Instructions for Temporaries.

KAREN'S COMPANY, INC.
234 West Main Street
Whereabouts, Ohio 44444
(614) 555-0000 Office
(614) 555-2233 Fax

STAFF LISTING

NAME	TITLE	EXTENSION
Anderson, James (Jim)	Sales Manager	430
Brown, Suzanne	Word Processing Supervisor	395
Carson, Doug	Personnel Manager	480
Chang, Danny	Systems Analyst	378
Clay, Roberta (Bobbie)	Operations Manager	438
Feinberg, Paul	Word Processor	350
Harrison, Judy	Customer Service Representative	356
Hayes, Brian	Accounting/Payroll Manager	427
Ives, Barbara	Administrative Assistant	320
Jaluski, Jan	Word Processor	340
Larrimer, Connie	Receptionist/Lobby	0
Mendenhall, Karen	President	360
Miller, Jerry	Graphics/Desktop Publishing	435
Pyles, Cindy	Word Processor	370
Romano, Diane	Secretary	345
Simpson, Larry	Customer Service Coordinator	415
Wilson, Teresa	Customer Service Representative	436

TELEPHONES — All incoming calls must be answered promptly and courteously. "Good Morning (Afternoon), Karen's Company." Ask the caller's name, company, and put them through. Managers' phones are programmed so that if they are on another line or out of their office, the call will be routed to the administrative assistant or secretary. On rare occasions, the call will come back to the switchboard, and you will take a message. Be certain to get the correct spelling of the caller's name, and the correct telephone number, including area code if it is long distance. If the caller says "I'm returning his call" or "She has my number," politely ask for it anyway. The only possible exception to this would be calls from family members. Even so, the message from the family member should indicate whether the person is calling from home or work.

JOB ORDERS AND CALLS FROM CLIENTS — Calls regarding what type of services we provide, prices/fees, time frames for completing projects, pending and/or new job requests should be given first to Larry Wilson (Customer Service Coordinator), then Judy Harrison (Customer Service Representative) or Teresa Wilson. If none of these people is available, give the call to Bobbie Clay (Operations Manager), or Karen Mendenhall

(President). It is essential that the caller be connected to someone ASAP — no exceptions. Never, ever, simply take a message from a client. There are no exceptions to this. This same procedure is to be followed for any walk-in clients. Ask them to have a seat in the lobby, and follow the protocol as far as notifying the appropriate staff member.

EMPLOYMENT APPLICATIONS — We occasionally get walk-in applicants. Blank applications are in the second drawer of the filing cabinet under "E" — for "Employment applications." These may be filled out in the reception area, or may be taken out of the office to be returned or mailed in later. Applicants may attach rsums. When applications are turned in, inform applicants that all applications are given to Doug Carson (Personnel Manager) for his review. Interviews are by appointment only; however, applicants are welcome to call Doug Carson to discuss employment possibilities.

SOLICITORS AND SALES REPRESENTATIVES — We discourage solicitors and sales representatives who do not have appointments. Tell solicitors that we are not interested, and tell sales representatives that they should call Bobbie Clay to arrange appointments. (She prefers to be called Bobbie, not Roberta.) If they want to leave business cards or brochures, put them in Bobbie's message slot. Do not attempt to answer questions about our company and do not get pulled into a discussion. Be polite, but firm. If you have a problem in this area, do not hesitate to notify Barbara Ives, Bobbie Clay, Doug Carson, or Karen Mendenhall. Any of us are happy to handle the situation.

MAIL/PACKAGE DELIVERIES — The mail is delivered and picked up once a day, usually between 9:00 A.M. and 10:00 A.M. Mail marked "personal" or "confidential" is not to be opened. Other mail is to be opened, stamped in, and placed in the mailboxes. When packages are delivered (UPS, Federal Express, etc.), call the person to whom the package is addressed and let him know he has a package. If the person is not at his desk, leave a note in his message slot, but continue to try to reach him. Notify Barbara Ives immediately when packages or letters (via messenger) are delivered for Karen Mendenhall.

MISCELLANEOUS — It is essential that the front desk be covered at all times. Do not leave the front desk unattended. There are no exceptions. Diane Romano and Barbara Ives relieve the receptionist for breaks, lunch, etc. They are both very conscientious about this. If they are not able to relieve you, they will see to it that someone else is. If you need to leave the area at times other than designated lunch and breaks, and you cannot reach either of these people, call Suzanne Brown, Jan Jaluski, or Cindy Pyles, in that order.

This is a sample. I realize that all companies are different. But this gives you a general idea of the type of information that is essential.

Depending on the structure of your organization, it may be necessary to provide a cross reference in addition to the alphabetical listing of names. For example:

ACCOUNTING DEPARTMENT		SHIPPING & RECEIVING DEPARTMENT	
Ames, Ann	2345	D'Amico, Joe	6789
Johnson, Tim	4567	Douglas, Pam	6543
Smith, Jason	3456	Temple, Roy	5432
Willis, Beth	5678	Conference Room	3229
		Copy Center	5334
		Computer Room	4226
		Lunchroom	4366
		Receptionist	0

The cross-referenced list is important because invariably callers will ask to be connected to the accounts payable department or customer service.

Be sure to include any special numbers and instructions for paging and car phones (if applicable).

Here are some other things to consider now that you know the essential things that must be done.

Saving(?) Money: Computers vs. Typewriters

Throughout 1990, 1991, and 1992, I listened to client companies emphasize their concerns about the recession and tight budgets. Let me first make it clear that I understand and applaud fiscal responsibility. But in the interest of saving a relatively small amount of money, many companies simply do not think things through—they don't use common sense. What business is that of mine and what on earth does it have to do with the subject of temporary employees?

A lot.

Several client companies I worked for requested a temporary to type documents on a typewriter. Even though they had computers and word processing software, they made it clear to the temporary help services that they did not want a "secretary" or a "word processor." What they really meant was that they did not want to *pay* a higher rate for someone to use word processing or computer skills.

OK—so they wanted to save money. Nothing wrong with that. But were they really saving money? Not necessarily. Since they required that documents (lengthy letters, reports, etc.) be typed on a typewriter, it took much longer to complete the jobs. It was often difficult or impossible to make any corrections to a document, especially after the page had been removed from the typewriter. So it had to be typed over again. Even for the most proficient typist who makes the keyboard sound like a machine gun, that takes time. Time is money.

A typical example is a six-day assignment where I was required to use a Xerox® MemoryWriter. Granted, most typewriters with memory are an improvement over standard typewriters, but they can't hold a candle to a good computer system. My supervisor was a very sweet elderly man who happened to have exceptional computer knowledge. This company had the latest software and computer equipment. I was given numerous lengthy documents to type. I could tell from the original I was given that the documents were form letters stored in the computer. But since my instructions were to type each original document on the typewriter, I had to type the complete text over and over again.

These were wordy, two-page form letters. A few variables within the text were changed for each letter. The client was adamant about not paying a higher rate to have the work done on the computer. During the course of the assignment, I heard many people bemoan company budget woes. They were tightening their belts, cutting back, being fiscally conscientious, etc., etc.

Obviously, this client did not save any money. Quite the contrary. The assignment was completed in six days. But doing the work on the computer would have taken no more than two and a half days, probably less than that. Without going into the specifics of what I was paid and what my temporary service charged the client, suffice it to say that in their efforts to save money, the client actually spent more money and made the work more difficult.

After the assignment ended, I calculated that the client had wasted $216.00. How did I reach that conclusion? Even at the lower rate of pay, my temporary service and I earned more on the six-day assignment than we would have earned on a three-day assignment. That was good for me and my service, but the client company did not "save" anything.

To this day, the man who insisted that I use the Xerox® MemoryWriter probably thinks he saved the company a couple of hundred dollars. This is just foolish — and this particular client should have known better.

Similar situations have happened more often than you would think. Clichés about forests and trees (and pennies and pounds) come to mind.

Travel Arrangements

A temporary will not know about personal preferences, special travel packages/promotions, price cut-offs, budgetary restrictions, credit cards, and billing procedures. This is another area where a mix-up that may or may not be the temporary's fault can spell disaster and embarrassment. It's better to have someone else take care of this unless the temporary is filling a long-term assignment.

Sufficient Work

See to it that the worker has enough to do. However, this does not mean that you should come to the temp worker every fifteen minutes and say, "Let me know when you run out of work to do." (Translation: We want to make sure that we get our money's worth.) It should be understood that *if* the temp finishes assigned projects quickly and needs more work, the supervisor or another *designated* person should be told.

Encourage Questions

If the worker is confused or not sure about how (or whether) to proceed with a task, make it clear that he should not hesitate to ask the supervisor. On the first day, check to see how things are going.

Time Cards

Most clients take care of time cards on the last day sometime after lunch and before the 5:00 exit from the building. (On Fridays, when the weather is nice, that exit turns into a stampede.) Understandably, a client is more reluctant to sign the time card before quitting time if they have gotten burned; i.e., if a temporary worker has ever gotten the card signed early and left the premises or goofed off the rest of the day. If this happens, call the service immediately.

It is perfectly all right to wait until the end of the day to sign the temporary employee's time card. But don't play power games with time cards. This is not the time for you to flex your power muscles. If you really need to bully a temporary employee or play your own version of "Time Card Torture" in order to make yourself look and feel important, you have some other serious problems.

CHECKLIST FOR EMPLOYERS

You think you need a temporary? You think you are ready to receive one in your office. Are you? This will help you pull it all together.

_____ One person has been assigned to introduce, train, and monitor work assignments.

_____ Other staff members in the area are aware that a temporary is coming, and it will be business as usual. No one is to dump his work on the temporary. If help is needed, they are to go through proper channels.

_____ A current, easy to read, alphabetical (last name first) list of names is available for the temporary to use. This is especially important if the temporary is going to be answering telephones.

_____ Instructions (preferably manuals) are available for machines (fax, copy machine, typewriters, tele phones, postage meter, etc.). In addition, basic telephone instructions should be written down, in cluding how to answer, transfer, and put on hold.

_____ The desk that the temp will be using is equipped with the necessary supplies, stationery, and envelopes.

_____ A map or diagram has been prepared which will enable the temporary worker to easily locate rest rooms, cafeteria, supply room, and other offices and departments that he/she will interact with or need access to.

_____ Coverage for the temp during breaks and lunch, if needed, has been pre-arranged.

_____ Samples of letters, memos, certain report formats, etc., are available for the temporary to use as a guideline.

This may seem like a lot of preparation and work, and maybe it is. But remember it only has to be done once, and updated only if there is a change in procedures and personnel. Taking care of the eight things on the above checklist will save you countless hours, many dollars, and much aggravation. It is well worth it.

IT ISN'T WORKING OUT—WHAT TO DO

So now you may be thinking: "Yeah, yeah. But what about the temporary who can't perform the simplest tasks, makes too many mistakes, and prefers to spend half the day chatting with other employees, talking to her kids on the telephone, and the other half in the break room smoking cigarettes and reading the newspaper?"

My question to you would be: Why are you putting up with someone like that? The only logical reasons would be: to reinforce the negative stereotype of temporary workers or maybe to justify the existence of your department and your own job. (See how busy we are? We are working incredibly hard, skipping lunches, and we still need extra help.) Perhaps you need a scapegoat. And a temporary scapegoat is better than no scapegoat at all.

If you are dissatisfied with a temporary worker, for any reason, you certainly have the right to end the assignment. Call the service as soon as possible and explain the problem. Are your expectations and requirements unreasonable? If not, make it clear to the service that you are not satisfied and that if a satisfactory replacement is not sent, you will take your temporary business elsewhere — permanently. Usually the service will jump through hoops to satisfy you and to maintain client goodwill.

Sometimes your problems are not solved by asking for a replacement from the same service or even by calling a different temporary help service. It is possible — though not probable—that the replacement will be worse, or have other (different) deficiencies and idiosyncrasies. For example, you may get someone who can type faster but doesn't have a pleasant telephone demeanor. Or maybe the quantity and quality of work are superior, but the temp's voice grates on your (and your clients') nerves.

Be aware that this street runs both ways. If temporaries don't like the assignment or if they are treated badly, they have the choice of sticking with it or terminating the assignment and moving on. Be careful about flexing your power

muscles, and if you get your jollies by "temporary bashing"
—watch out. More simply put, the temp can dump *you* and/or
badmouth your place of business. It happens every day.

If you have a negative experience with a temporary employee, please do not generalize and assume that the entire
industry is as unsatisfactory. One factor that contributes to
the negative image of temporary employees and the services
they work for is that a client may have had one or more bad
experiences with former temps. Perhaps the temporary help
service(s) they dealt with were not professional or were even
downright flaky.

One or two bad apples can indeed spoil the bunch. But
neither the temporary service industry in general nor temporary employees in particular should be blamed for one bad
experience, or even several bad experiences.

Think of it this way: If your car breaks down, do you
abandon it on the side of the road and resolve never to drive
again? Nope. If your roof leaks, do you give up on living in
houses or apartments? I doubt it. If you discover that the
dress or suit you bought doesn't fit or that you simply don't
like it, do you stop wearing clothes and run naked through
the streets? Of course not. You return the merchandise,
choose something else, or get a refund. You might badmouth
that brand, style, or even a particular store, but you shop
around. Apply that same strategy to temporary help services. If you are not satisfied with the worker and/or the
service, *dump them*. And move on to another one. Don't
generalize and label the entire industry based on a small
sample.

Karen, You're Fired!

As of this writing, there have been two occasions when
an employer expressed dissatisfaction, called the temporary
help company, and terminated me.

A prestigious philanthropic foundation needed someone to
fill in for the executive secretary to the President for two
weeks while she went on vacation. The client requested that I
stop by for a few minutes the day prior to the beginning of the
assignment to meet the man to whom I would be reporting.
This was not a real orientation, and there was little discussion of the job duties. Instead, the time was spent giving me a
tour of the opulent building and impressing on me the importance of the foundation and its visitors.

I was told that due to the nature of the business, the
President always took his calls directly, and that I was only

to take the President's calls when he was on the phone or out of the building. I was cautioned by the regular secretary that the President would try to intimidate me, and that I shouldn't let it get to me.

Things went well the first day. The next workday, I ran out of work to do early in the afternoon. After asking the other secretary if I could help her and learning that she was working on something that she had to do herself, I asked the President, my supervisor, if he had any work for me to do. His reaction was odd. He was visibly irritated by my question and went to several people to find out if they had excess work. No one did. He then went into his office and closed the door. About a half hour later, he brought out a tape for me to transcribe.

I had difficulty understanding a portion of the tape and asked him for clarification. He told me to guess as he "had no idea what (I was) talking about." I proceeded to type the letter to the best of my ability. A few minutes later, he yelled from his office, "Do you have it done yet?" I said "almost."

He immediately came out to my desk and stood with his hands on his hips. He wanted to let me and everyone else know that I was making him wait. He said, very loudly, "I need it now." I had not proofed the letter and had not run a spellcheck on the word processor. I made a judgment call and punched in the command to print it. This man actually went over to the printer and started pulling on the document, jamming the printer. He then looked at it and said, very loudly, "Look at this. You made two spelling errors. You should proofread your work. I am spoiled. I am used to getting things fast and perfect."

On the morning of the third day of the assignment, the hostile behavior continued. He screamed at the main lobby receptionist for not sending his calls to me, although it had been made clear to everyone that his calls were to be given to no one but him. Later in the day, he left the office being uncharacteristically pleasant. He was whistling and smiling and said to me, "Please try to get as much done today as you can. I'll be in tomorrow around 2:00—see you then."

At 6:00 that evening, I received a call at home from my assignment coordinator. She said that the client had called her early that morning to request that I be terminated because the President was dissatisfied with my productivity level. I gave her my side of the story, and expressed concern that I had not been informed hours earlier. As it turns out, I was the last to know that I was being let go. The client did not want a replacement; they decided to make do until the regular secretary returned from her vacation.

It seemed clear to me and my service, that I was not at fault. They said that they had expressed surprise to the client and told him that I had worked on many assignments for them and they had received only excellent evaluations from my supervisors. I received another assignment right away.

Soon after that incident, I received a call from another temporary. This lady has superior skills and works exclusively for one service. We discussed some of the ups and downs of temp life. She mentioned that she had recently been fired from a temp assignment. I laughed and told her what had happened to me. We both found consolation in the knowledge that it happens to the best of us and that we both received other assignments immediately.

The other time that I was fired was from a small law firm. This firm had been through a series of temporaries over the course of a year. Some had quit after a short stint, others stayed longer, and a few had been terminated. I was filling two vacant slots for an indefinite period of time. After I had been on the assignment for four months, one of the attorneys told me that he considered it an intrusion for me to bring letters into his office for him to sign. The office manager had explicitly asked me to take the letters in to him in the way I had been doing. This was indicative of an ongoing power struggle at the firm. The attorney for whom I worked would give me one set of instructions, and the office manager would tell me to do something else entirely the moment the attorney walked away. I asked for clarification, but rarely received a response.

One Friday afternoon at ten minutes until 5:00 I received a call from my coordinator telling me that the client had asked for a replacement. She said they had decided they were dissatisfied with my production level, and had requested I not be told until the end of the day. The day I was terminated, both my supervisors had bolted out the door earlier in the afternoon without saying one word to me. I turned my office key over to another employee, told her I had been terminated, made certain things were in order, and removed my hand lotion and tissues from the desk. As I left the office, I made sure that the door didn't hit me in the derriere.

During my four months on this assignment, I had never been late nor absent. I had been filling two vacant positions, coming in early to open the office, cranking out hundreds of documents, and working overtime when required. There had been some exasperating moments, but I did not express frustration about anything or anyone. Being terminated came as a complete surprise.

If you (the employer) are dissatisfied, you certainly have the right to end the assignment. There are, of course, various ways to handle the termination, some more professional than others. The above situations could have been better handled. For example, the clients should have approached me directly, either before or after calling the temporary help service.

Taking the time to say something simple directly to the temporary worker is a more responsible action. Simply saying, "Karen, things aren't working out the way that we would like. Although we appreciate the work you have done, the assignment will end today. We would like for you to finish the day," would have made a big difference. To call the temporary help company early in the day and ask the coordinator to wait until the end of the day to inform the temporary employee is a sloppy way to conduct business.

IT WORKED OUT GREAT—WHAT TO DO

Frequently (I hope), you will have some experiences with temporary workers that exceed your best expectations. A "supertemp" saved the day, or the week. Perhaps the worker did a bang-up job and cheerfully handled tasks you usually have to give to two or three permanent workers. Or maybe the temp's personality and disposition contributed that extra special something which improved the work atmosphere.

If the coordinator from the temporary help service calls to see how things are going, let them know that they sent you a terrific person. But if the service doesn't call you, call them. And when the assignment ends, follow up with a written complimentary letter. It won't take much of your time. (I'll prove it to you.)

```
                                      September 10, 19XX

Jan Porter
XYZ Temporary Services
1234 East Horizon Dr., Suite 202
Columbus, OH 40000-1111

RE: Teresa Todd

Dear Jan:
    I wanted to take a moment to thank you for sending Teresa
to us. I admit that I was apprehensive about the idea of hav-
ing a stranger replace my Executive Secretary, but my fears
soon disappeared.
    Teresa caught on to the procedures with very little in-
struction. She cranked out an incredible amount of work. This
was great, because no one had much time to spend with her. In
addition to top-notch skills, Teresa's pleasant disposition
improved the general office atmosphere. I received several
compliments from staff and clients about the quality of her
work and her demeanor.
    If we ever have the need for temporary services in the fu-
ture, I will call you.
    Thanks again——Teresa Todd was a lifesaver.

Very truly yours,



Richard P. Simms
Vice President
```

It took me exactly eight minutes to compose and type that letter.

Several clients have written complimentary letters about my performance to the services I have worked for. I mention this only because they came as complete surprises to me. It is interesting to note that on some assignments where I worked like a dog, went the extra mile, and was not treated particularly well, the attitude of some of the clients and other people at the work site was: "Temporaries are a dime a dozen. Make sure that door doesn't knock you down on your way out."

A letter of thanks can also be in the form of a "To Whom It May Concern" reference letter given directly to the temporary worker, or a letter addressed to the temporary help company. Give a copy of the letter to the temp. It may go a long way in helping the person get a job at some point in the future.

A "thank you" is nice, but when a worker does a really sensational job, it doesn't hurt a bit for you to take a moment and go the extra mile to help him/her out or just to be nice.

I accepted an assignment filling in for one week for a secretary who was on vacation. This was a large company that I didn't know much about. The pay rate was low, but I needed the work. I wasn't too excited about spending the week answering phones and typing on a typewriter. But I decided to make the most of it. I'm glad I did. Everything kind of fell into place. The people were so nice that I wanted to do a super job for them, and I did.

On the first day they mentioned the computer software programs they used. I volunteered the fact that I was a computer junkie, and they seemed interested. However, I told them (in a very nice way) that if they wanted me to do correspondence, etc., on the computer, I would have to inform the temporary help service, and there would be a rate adjustment. The client didn't want to go that route — they were satisfied with my work on the Xerox® MemoryWriter.

In the course of the week they discussed the conversion of some documents from one word processing package to a different one. I knew a simple way to accomplish that task and volunteered brief instructions on how to do it — no strings attached. This didn't take much of my time, and saved them much time and money. They appreciated the information and made sure I felt their appreciation.

I have met some absolutely terrific people while working at temporary assignments. One place gave me a party even though I only worked there two weeks. I had done an exceptional job for them, and the working chemistry was great. At another assignment, my supervisor brought me a box of gourmet chocolate chip cookies to show that he appreciated my help. I had come in on short notice and cranked out a lot of work in a few hours. Many clients have taken me out to lunch on my last day. And yes, I have received more than my share of cakes and flowers. Mind you, I never expected any types of "gratuities." But they are great.

I'm not suggesting that you go to a lot of expense, shut down operations, call a catering service, rent a hotel suite, and throw a huge farewell party. There are limits. You have work to do. But it doesn't hurt to make some type of gesture of appreciation if the situation merits it.

One excruciatingly conservative, serious minded, nose to the grindstone partner of a law firm wrote me several notes on projects that I typed for him: "Good job!" (with a drawing of a smiling face), "Another great job!" He knew how hard I had labored over those documents, and my workload was nearly impossible at that assignment. But those little notes made me feel good. Of course, he was a tough taskmaster. I also know for a fact that writing little notes wasn't his normal style. He went the extra mile to make a difficult job assignment bearable and also to make my day a bit more pleasant. Now that's class.

Call it what you like, but there is no denying that those little notes motivated me to work harder, though I was ready to drop from sheer exhaustion at the end of the day. Further proof that you can indeed "catch more flies with honey ..."

Unlike permanent employees, temporary workers really don't expect bonuses. They don't demand perks, benefits, and "exciting, challenging, intrinsically rewarding work with growth opportunities." All they expect—and rightly so—is a paycheck that they have earned for services rendered. That is usually all they get; it's an even exchange. It is always a nice surprise to receive something extra.

MAKING A TEMPORARY A PERMANENT FIXTURE

If the worker is an independent contractor or is working for you on an informal, freelance basis, you can hire the person as soon as you want (if they accept).

However, if the employee was sent to you by a temporary help company, there are several factors to be considered. First of all, I don't advise entering into any hiring agreement without discussing it with the temporary service that placed the temporary employee in the job. Temporary help companies usually have strict, explicit, written policies regarding permanent hiring of their workers. Often those policies are stated on the client copy of the time card. A typical example is:

    The client acknowledges the considerable expense incurred
    by ABC Temporary Services, Inc. to advertise, recruit,
    reference check, and retain their temporary employees. We
    are pleased when a client wants to hire one of our tem-
    poraries as a permanent employee. However, it is under-
    stood that in consideration of the services provided by
    ABC Temporary Services, Inc., the client agrees that in
    the event the employee named on this time card is hired
    by the client within 90 days from the first day of em-
    ployment as a temporary, the client shall pay a fee of

$_____ as a separation expense. By signing this time
card, you agree to those terms, confirm the hours worked
at your company for the designated pay period, authorize
ABC Temporary Services, Inc. to pay the temporary employee
and to issue you an invoice for services rendered.

Each individual situation is different, but usually an ami-
cable separation agreement can be worked out. Make certain
you understand the policy. The client company may be required to pay a lump sum fee or to sign an agreement to
keep the employee on as a temporary employee for a certain
period of time while paying the service an hourly rate. Remember that temporary help services spend considerable
time and money recruiting, testing, evaluating, and marketing their employees.

Some temporary services do not charge the client company any fee whatsoever when a worker is hired permanently. The reasoning behind that is they want to maintain
a good relationship with a valued client. This can be especially true if the client is using other temporaries from that
service on a regular basis.

I AM ON YOUR SIDE (REALLY)

You may feel that I am asking too much of you, but I'm not. If
you pay attention to the tips provided, you will save yourself
and your company a lot of time, money, and headache. This
particular chapter, directed at employers, was the seed for
this book. This is where it all began. As the author, naturally
I feel that every word I have written is important. But the
chapter you have just finished is, by far, the most crucial.

You might disagree with some (or all) of the things I
have said. You may be uncomfortable, even angry, at being
faced with some things that you would rather not have
pointed out to you. But I'll close this chapter by telling you
something else, and I promise it won't hurt one bit:

You, the client, have the right to insist on professionalism, courtesy, competence, efficiency, and adherence to your
rules and regulations from temporary help services and
temporary employees. Don't ever settle for anything less.

See? I told you I was on your side.

10

Comments from Industry Experts

QUALITIES OF THE IDEAL TEMPORARY WORKER

I asked the assignment coordinators at a reputable temporary help company what they would identify as the most important qualities of the ideal temporary. Their "single most important factor above all others" was dependability. Adaptability was a close second. In addition, they said:

We have a very high caliber clientele. We demand top skills. But typing X-number of words per minute isn't enough. Of course, we expect good skills. We also look at other things that may come across to us during the interview and during our association with the temporary employee. Our "stars" have savvy, polish, a professional attitude, common sense, and a select few have "that certain something" that makes them winners. They are personable, articulate, they know how to conduct themselves in different types of office atmospheres. They know the secrets of getting along with different types of personalities. They know how to "handle" difficult people and touchy situations. A sense of humor always helps. A "Super-temp" does not call us and whine about minor inconveniences, but he or she is smart enough to make us aware of a situation that may be a problem. The winner will go in and do what needs to be done.

MY FAVORITE TEMPORARY HELP COMPANY

Abby Lane/Dana Temporaries, Inc. in Columbus, Ohio provides temporary and permanent job placement services.

Dana Geary is the Vice President. Prior to setting up her own business in 1988, Dana worked on a few temporary assignments to get a feel for what it is like. I only wish that more temporary help companies would periodically send their staff out into the trenches.

Throughout this book I have referred to "my favorite service." Although I have had great relationships with many temporary help companies, Abby Lane/Dana Temporaries, Inc. gets the prize. They specialize in providing support staff for law firms (legal secretaries, receptionists, and paralegals); however, their clientele also includes other business sectors such as insurance companies, engineering firms, and advertising agencies. The staff is small, thereby permitting a more personal touch with temporary employees and client companies. The clientele is top notch, and, although I have liked certain job assignments more than others, they have never sent me on a "crummy" job assignment. The staff at Abby Lane/Dana has always worked hard to keep me working.

One thing that sets Abby Lane/Dana Temporaries, Inc. apart from many temporary services is that they don't simply put a warm body in a slot in order to earn a fee. Skills and personalities are carefully considered and matched accordingly. If they don't have someone available to suit the client's needs at that particular time, the client is told. And if there is no job assignment available at a particular time, the staff will be up front about it and tell the temporary employee.

This service goes to bat for their temps. They work hard to get the best pay rate and working conditions for their employees. It is unusual for a temporary help service to risk losing a client in order to keep a temporary employee happy, but this service has gone out on a limb for me many times.

I have been working for Abby Lane/Dana Temporaries since 1990, and I waited for a long time before I revealed my book project to Dana. When I felt the time was right, I told her that I wanted to get her comments about various aspects of the industry. Here are my questions and her comments.

Q. What are some of the qualities of the "ideal" temporary employee?

A. Punctuality, flexibility, and a willingness to go on an assignment, of any nature, on short notice.

Q. If a temporary complains about being mistreated by a client company, how is it handled?

A. If the client is clearly at fault, I will not send any more temporaries to that client.

Q. Do you have any additional comments about the temporary services industry?

A. I think that in today's economy, temporaries are in demand. For businesses that cannot, for budget reasons, hire permanent employees, temporary services are the answer.

COMMENTS FROM NATS

I presented a situational example and a couple of questions to a spokesman for NATS in Alexandria, Virginia. Here are my questions and his responses.

Q. The temporary is unhappy with the assignment. The service misrepresented the job. The people at the work site are nasty and their expectations are unreasonable. The temp has spoken with the temporary help service several times and complained. The service says they don't have anything else (a replacement assignment) and they advise the temporary to "stick it out." They even offer more money. But the temp is still miserable.

How should this situation be handled? Is a temporary employee ever justified in "walking off" a job assignment?

A. Yes, there are some instances in which a temporary employee would be justified to "walk." If a client company makes demands in which a temporary employee feels that their personal safety is compromised, they most certainly should NOT continue in such an assignment. If a client company is misrepresenting the job assignment, the temporary help company should be notified. In addition, obviously a temporary employee must never be asked to do something that is illegal. In all instances, the employee has a responsibility and obligation to report any abuses to the temporary help company.

A temporary employee should be treated with the equal amount of respect that a company extends to all its regular, full-time employees. Although NATS feels that a temporary employee does have the obligation to complete an assignment once accepted, if that assignment was misrepresented, then the temporary employee is within his/her rights to give notice. If the assignment situation is just too untenable, then the temporary employee must make a personal decision based upon their need for income versus their own discomfort.

Q. Does NATS ever receive complaints about temporary employees or temporary help companies? If so, what type of action (if any) is taken?

A. As a trade association which represents the temporary help industry, we do not receive complaints about specific temporary employees. It is up to the client company and the temporary help company to resolve any such grievances.

When a temporary help company joins NATS (which represents 85% of the industry based upon total U.S. sales volume), they agree to abide by our published Code of Ethics. NATS does have a formal grievance procedure, which in the twenty-six-year history of our association, has rarely been used. Legally, for antitrust reasons, the only action we could take (although, to the best of our knowledge this has never occurred) would be to deny membership based upon this non-compliance with our published Code of Ethics.

TOMORROW'S FORECAST

As stated earlier in this book, in March of 1992 the U.S. Department of Labor reported that more than nine million people in the United States were unemployed. The unemployment rate was 7.3% (higher than it has been for seven years). Thousands of people have been victims of down-sizing, lay-offs, and companies going out of business.

In the area where I live and work there was a decline in job orders and job assignments in late 1990 through 1991. I noticed a rebound after the Persian Gulf crisis ended. And in 1992, many of the temporary help companies I worked for agreed that business was considerably better than it was in 1990 and 1991.

According to NATS, with the exception of the period before and during the recession (which "officially" began in mid-1990), the temporary help industry has enjoyed a healthy growth rate over the last decade. Future trends, however, should reflect a more moderate growth pattern than experienced in previous years. The industry is expected to grow 2% to 8% a year through the year 2000.

A spokesman for NATS explains how the temporary help industry can serve as a barometer of the nation's economy: *Historic patterns have emerged over the last twenty years that show the temporary help industry is negatively affected prior to the onset of economic downturn and/or a recession. This is because our industry has a tendency to cycle a little ahead of business activity and, therefore, the general economy.*

The bottom line is that temporary employees are going to be around for a long time to come.

Epilogue

I started out with the intention of writing a short article directed at employers to submit to magazines for publication consideration. Then I became excited about—at times even obsessed with—the project. It has been a lot of hard work. But I have loved every minute of it, and I never once thought of giving up. Regardless of whether you bought, borrowed, or ran across this book, the fact that you are holding this book in your hands right now means that all those hours, days, nights, weekends spent at the library and at home in front of my computer were worth it.

Being human, we all make mistakes. Even a veteran temporary employee with as much mileage as I have accumulated makes mistakes and errors in judgment. Throughout this book I share my experiences and those of other temporaries and client companies with you. I will spare you the clichés about hindsight, but I admit there are a few situations that I wish I had handled differently. Sure, I had to learn some lessons the hard way. But I am proud that I always gave it my best shot.

As I worked on my manuscript, I continued to work at temporary assignments. And I now feel better about my temporary tribulations. I hope the same applies to you.

One last thing: Remember that quiz I gave you at the beginning of Chapter 1? Go back and ask yourself the question again. After reading this book, you now realize that the correct answer is #3. You should be more worried about running out of coffee than about working with a temporary employee.

NATS Lexicon of Terms

To improve understanding of the temporary help business and to help distinguish it from fundamentally different businesses such as the employment agency business and employee leasing, NATS has prepared this glossary, their "Lexicon of Terms."

AGENCY—An employment agency (see Employment Agency).

APPLICANT—An individual seeking temporary employment with a temporary help company. In the employment agency business, "applicant" means a person seeking to be permanently placed.

ASSIGN—The act of sending a temporary employee to work on the premises of a customer of the temporary help company. "Assign" is different from "refer" which describes the employment agency practice of sending an applicant to a prospective employer for an interview. "Refer" and "referral" do not apply to the act of assigning temporary employees.

ASSIGNMENT—The period of time during which a temporary employee is working on a customer's premises.

COMMINGLING—See Joint Operations.

COORDINATOR—The staff employee of a temporary help company who assigns temporary employees to work on the customer's premises.

COUNSELOR — An employment agency employee who refers or places applicants for employment with employers. The term does not apply to a staff employee of a temporary help company. Many state employment agency laws require that counselors be licensed.

CUSTOMER — The person, organization, or business that uses the service of a temporary help company.

DISPATCH—The term is generally used to refer to the act of assigning industrial temporary employees to report for work on customer's premises.

EMPLOYEE LEASING—An arrangement whereby a business transfers its employees to the payroll of a "leasing organization" after which the employees are leased back to their original employer where they continue working in the same capacity as before in an ongoing, permanent relationship.

EMPLOYMENT AGENCY—A business whose purpose is to bring a job seeker and a prospective employer together for the purpose of effecting a permanent employment relationship.

FEE — The amount charged by an employment agency for placing job seekers in permanent positions. The term does not refer to a temporary help company's gross profit or liquidated damages charge. (See Liquidated Damages.)

GENERAL EMPLOYER—An employer who has the right to hire and fire an employee, is responsible for the employee's wages and benefits, and exercises ultimate supervision, discipline, and control over the employee. Temporary help companies are the general employers of their temporary employees. (See Special Employer.)

IN-HOUSE TEMPORARY—An individual hired directly by a non temporary help company as a permanent employee to perform various temporary assignments within that company.

INDEPENDENT CONTRACTOR — A person, not an employee, who performs work for another. Unlike employees, independent contractors: (1) are not subject to the control and supervision of the person using the services regarding the details of how the work is to be performed, (2) generally have specialized training or education, and (3) supply all necessary tools, supplies, or equipment necessary to perform the work.

JOB ORDER—See Work Order.

JOB SHOP — A colloquial term generally used to refer to businesses that supply longer term temporary employees on a contract basis in technical or specialized areas such as engineering, drafting, etc.

JOINT OPERATIONS— The operation of both a temporary help company and an employment agency by the same firm. Problems arise when these fundamentally different operations are conducted with the same personnel, forms, and procedures so that the two businesses are not easily distinguished by job applicants and customers. Such "commingling" leads to public confusion about the nature of the temporary help business and could subject the industry to employment agency regulation. To avoid confusion, NATS has developed guidelines to help NATS members keep the two businesses separate.

LIQUIDATED DAMAGES—Liquidated damages are monies paid by temporary help customers under agreements in which the customer agrees not to hire the temporary employee within some specified period of time and to pay damages for breach of that promise in the agreed upon (i.e., "liquidated") amount.

PART-TIME—A work period less than the full work-day or full work-week. "Part-time" employees are not "temporary" employees because, unlike temporary employees, they work a regular schedule for their employer on an ongoing, indefinite basis. (See Temporary Employee.)

PAYROLLING—A colloquial term in the temporary help industry that describes a situation whereby the customer, rather than the temporary help company, recruits an individual and asks the temporary help company to consider employing the individual and assigning him to the customer on a temporary basis. Once hired by the temporary help company, the "payrolled" employee's employment relationship with the temporary help company is the same as any other temporary employee.

PLACEMENT—An employment agency term describing the act of successfully placing a job seeker in a permanent position with an employer.

SPECIAL EMPLOYER—A term referring to a customer's legal relationship to the temporary employees assigned to them. The relationship is based on the customer's right to direct and control the specific details of the work to be performed. As "special employers," customers have certain legal rights and obligations regarding temporary employees. For example, because worker's compensation insurance (which temporary help companies provide for their employees) is the exclusive relief available to employees against "employers" for work-related injuries, a temporary employee generally cannot sue his "special employer" (the customer) for negligence. Hence, the customer's special employer status insulates it from such liability. On the other hand, as special employers, customers may also have certain obligations to temporary employees, e.g., not to discriminate against them in violation of the civil rights laws. (See General Employer.)

SUPPLEMENTAL STAFFING — This term generally refers to the practice of supplementing the permanent staff of hospitals, nursing homes, and other health care staff with personnel employed by temporary help companies.

TEMP-TO-PERM — (Also referred to as "Try before you hire") The practice of sending temporary employees on an assignment for the express purpose of ultimately placing them in a permanent position with the customer. his is an employment agency activity which may subject a temporary help company to regulation under state employment laws. "Temp-to-perm" practices include but are not limited to:

Advertising "temp-to-perm" positions to attract workers seeking permanent jobs.

Suggesting or recommending to customers that they use temporary employees on a "temp-to-perm" basis.

Agreeing to customers' requests to send temporary employees to the customer on a "temp-to-perm" basis.

Sending temporary employees to customers to be interviewed for the purpose of determining who will be assigned to the customer on a "temp-to-perm" basis.

TEMPORARY EMPLOYEE — An employee who does not make a commitment to an employer to work on a regular, ongoing basis but instead is free to accept (or reject) assignments at such times and for such length of time as the employee may choose. A temporary employee is obligated only to complete a particular assignment once one is accepted, but has no obligation to accept further assignments. (See Part-Time Employee.)

TEMPORARY HELP COMPANY — An organization engaged in the business service of furnishing its own employees ("temporaries") to handle customers' temporary staffing needs and special projects.

TRY BEFORE YOU HIRE — See Temp-to-perm.

WORK ORDER — An order received from a customer for a temporary help company's services. In the employment agency industry, the term "Job Order" refers to a request from a prospective employer authorizing the employment agency to find an appropriate prospective employee.

Index